"Going to the Pictures" was one of the nation's favourite pastimes in the first sixty years of this century, but until now was an activity largely ignored by historians. Now Janet McBain, Curator of the Scottish Film Archive, has written the first-ever account of what it was like to own, work in, or simply patronise, Scotland's cinemas in days gone by. From the owners of whole chains of picture houses, to the lowly-paid lads and lasses who helped work the projectors or sold confectionery, the author has recorded oral evidence of the bygone cinema industry and its public to present a unique compendium of memories of Scotland's

"Pictures Past"

Green's Playhouse, Glasgow, shortly after opening in 1927.

# PICTURES PAST

Recollections of
Scottish cinemas
and cinema-going

By
Janet McBain
Archivist, Scottish Film Council

MOORFOOT PUBLISHING
EDINBURGH     1985

ISBN 0 906606 12 8

**British Library Cataloguing in Publication Data**
McBain, Janet
  Pictures past : recollections of Scottish cinemas
and cinema-going.
  1. Moving-picture theatres — Scotland — History
  I. Title
  791.43′09411    PN1993.5.G7

The publisher acknowledges subsidy from
the Scottish Arts Council towards
publication of this volume

Published by:
  Moorfoot Publishing,
  PO Box 506,
  SW Postal District,
  Edinburgh 10

Printed by:
  Kelso Graphics,
  The Knowes,
  Kelso.

# CONTENTS

Jimmy Nairn painting the Playhouse foyer as a Christmas fairyland.

This book is dedicated
to the memory of
Jimmy Nairn
doyen of cinema managers,
remembered with affection
by colleagues and patrons
alike.

# FOREWORD

This is the history of cinema-going in Scotland from the first-hand experiences of those who owned and ran cinemas, the employees who staffed the hundreds of picture houses and the patrons who regularly attended their local "bug hut" and picture palace.

It is not another general history of the film industry in this country, nor is it an analysis of the art of the film. Some attention is paid to the architecture of the cinemas, as is some mention made of the supply of films and the events that influenced the production side of the industry, but only as a backdrop, to set into their context the personal experiences of the contributors.

Cinema was, in its day, one of the most popular forms of entertainment the world has known. Scots, like their contemporaries worldwide, went to the pictures in their thousands. As Christopher Harvie says in his definitive history of modern Scotland *No Gods and Precious Few Heroes* (Edward Arnold, ed. Jenny Wormald):

> "To the Scots the movies were magic. In 1950
> Glasgow people went on average 51 times a year,
> and Scots as a whole 36 times, while the English
> paid only 28 visits."

With so much collective memory of picture-going, it would be impossible to relate everybody's recollections. Readers will have stories of their own to add to those provided here, and they may take issue with some of the opinions expressed. All to the good. But, if this is to become a memory that future generations can continue to enjoy, it has to be preserved. Please, if you have something to offer which will add to our knowledge of cinema in Scotland, get in touch with me at the Scottish Film Archive. It may be personal recollections or perhaps film, photographs, or cinema memorabilia. We are particularly keen to hear from those whose memories touch on the silent era and from women who worked as projectionists in wartime.

Janet McBain

Scottish Film Archive,
74 Victoria Crescent Road,
Glasgow,
G12 9JN.

William Walker filming the Braemar Gathering, 1898

## PART 1. THE MOVIES COME TO SCOTLAND

Contrary to her normal opinion of contemporary society, Queen Victoria certainly was "amused" by moving pictures when they were first presented to her at Balmoral Castle in 1898. Her Majesty's interest had been aroused by local cinematographer William Walker, who had been seen filming the recent Braemar Gathering. In response to a royal request, Walker gave a Command Performance of this and the rest of his cinematograph programme at Balmoral on 24th October 1898, and it was to herald a series of visits to Queen Victoria's summer retreat over the ensuing years. Her Majesty, obviously taken with the novelty, had conferred upon the Aberdonian the right to call his company Walker's "Royal" Cinematograph.

William Walker had embarked upon his film-making interests some two years previously by acquiring the revolutionary new invention of a cinematograph projector and a stock of short films to add to his existing optical lantern business. He was so quickly convinced of the success of moving images that soon afterwards he purchased a film camera and started up a small venture in making films of local events and showing them in towns and villages all over the north-east. The idea caught on and Walker employed two local men, Paul Robello and later Joe Gray, to assist him with the business, taking pictures of a variety of events such as the Lord Provost's Garden Party, the Highland Brigade at Gordon Castle and Aberdeen harbour during a storm.

Walker was one of a growing band of entrepreneurs convinced of the attraction of the "flickers" which by the mid-1890s were appearing as side shows in fairground booths, in public halls, at magic lantern lectures and in variety and music halls.

It is difficult to say precisely when the Scots first had an opportunity to see these early films as several rival claims and very little documentary evidence confuse the issue. From the earliest days, the travelling showmen took cinematographs with them as another novelty for their fairground amusements and sideshows, and to them must be given credit for taking moving pictures to the far corners of the land. Certainly Scotland's first recorded public screening of films in an established place of entertainment had a disappointing beginning. The American Edison's Kinetoscope, adapted from its peep-show ancestor, failed to thrill the Edinburgh audience at the Empire Palace Theatre in Nicolson Street when it was shown to them on 13th April, 1896. According to contemporary accounts, the lighting was poor and the pictures dull. Fortunately, there was a good variety programme to compensate.

Over the next few months, some of the technical hitches were overcome and rival systems all made their debut to the public. The Lumière Brothers' Cinematographe arrived in Glasgow a few weeks later, and by September Britain's version, invented by Robert Paul, had hit the headlines in Aberdeen. By the end of 1896, it was possible to see moving pictures in most towns and many villages in Scotland.

It was to be some time, however, before permanent homes would be found for films. They were still regarded as a novelty to be enjoyed as part of a fairground entertainment or to fill in time between live acts at the variety theatres. In the ensuing years, public halls were leased for weekly shows and various Cinematograph or Bioscope companies toured the outlying areas with film and musical programmes.

Heading the rush for rented shops and commercial premises for the showing of cinematographs were Hales Tours, recreating the thrills of a railway journey. Patrons were seated in a mock railway carriage which rocked and swayed whilst ahead on the screen the scenery was seen to fly past, filmed by a camera mounted on the front of a locomotive. T.J. West's Modern Marvel Company offered similar fare and proved exceedingly popular in Lowland towns.

In addition to the intense competition between the various operators the fledgling cinema industry had to compete with an even newer craze, roller skating. Its popularity was to last a decade into the new century. Looking down on all this from an aloof

Lumiere's projection apparatus in use.                    *Science Museum*

# PROGRAMME

— OF —

# CINEMATOGRAPH

— AND —

## OPTICAL LANTERN EXHIBITION

— AT —

 BALMORAL CASTLE.

Monday, 24th October, 1898.

Programme for the first Royal Command Performance

# Programme

Between the Cinematographs, Floral and Classical Tableaux and Dioramic Effects will be displayed.

SCOTLAND FOR EVER—
Scots Greys and Gordon Highlanders.

METROPOLITAN FIRE BRIGADE SCENES—
Off to the Fire.
House on Fire.

CINDERELLA—
The Fairy Godmother and Ballroom Scenes.

THE MARCH OF THE CAMERON MEN.

VOLLEY FIRING AND CHARGE OF THE CAMERONS.

TRAIN SCENES—
Train entering and emerging from Tunnel.
The Scotch Express.

LIVELY PILLOW FIGHT BY CHILDREN.

TRAIN ARRIVING AT BALLATER.

BRAEMAR GATHERING AT BALMORAL—
March Past of the Clans.
Balmoral Highlanders (The Queen's Own).
The Duff, Farquharson, and Forbes Men.
Strathspey and Reel.

THE BAKER AND THE SWEEP.

BUTTERFLY DANCE.

THE LONDON SCOTTISH—
Entry into Perth.

CURLING AND SKATING AT GLENMUICK.

BANCHORY FROM THE RAILWAY.

THE PHOTOGRAPHER AND THE GHOST.

HIGHLAND FLING BY CHILDREN.

BRITISH TOURISTS IN CAIRO.

SWORD DANCE.

THE CONJUROR.

SNOWBALLING.

ABERDEEN HOSPITAL SATURDAY—
Comic Costume Cycle Parade.

CAVALRY TOURNAMENT—
Steeplechase.
Cavalry to the Front.

AT THE PANTOMIME.

RULE BRITANNIA.

National Anthem.

of Walker's Cinematograph at Balmoral Castle, 24th October, 1898.

Poster advertising a cinematograph performance in the Public Hall, Uphall, 1903.

*Scottish Record Office*

position, "respectable" Victorian society could confidently dismiss moving pictures as a nine day wonder.

In the early 1900s, the "penny gaffs" suddenly mushroomed. Converted hastily from shops, roller rinks and factory premises, into primitive and not always sanitary film theatres, they did little to enhance the reputation of the cinema as a diversion for the masses. Not surprisingly then, some of the earliest full-time cinemas were located away from the city centres in the predominantly working class districts. By the end of the Edwardian era, however, attempts to elevate the lowly status of cinema began to be reflected in the construction of rather more comfortable and well appointed picture halls in the centres of towns and cities. With padded seats, a pianist and in some cases, tearooms, a more genteel class of patron was encouraged to attend.

As demand increased, particularly after the First World War, larger and more luxurious halls were built. These picture palaces, seating thousands at a time, sprang up all over the country. The cinema had become respectable.

## PART 2. THE EXHIBITORS

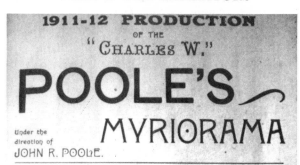

Poster advertising Poole's Myriorama

*J.K.S. Poole*

## 1) POOLES OF EDINBURGH

The showmen who toured the country with fairground and novelty shows must be given great credit for helping to establish the popularity of the cinema and for stamping the industry with the ingenuity and imagination that film exhibition was later to display in the heyday of its popularity.

Most towns have associations with one or more show families. Names like Codona, Macindoe, Leo, Wilmot and Biddall all conjure up recollections of fairs, freak shows, roundabouts and bustling excitement. Many of the most successful and enduring family businesses in cinema in Scotland had their orgins in the travelling shows and by following their story, it helps to chart the rise of the industry from its humble peripatetic origins.

In Edinburgh, the name of Poole is synonymous with cinema, particularly coupled with the Synod Hall. However, this family business had begun several decades before films first appeared there in the early 1900s. Their speciality was the great panorama, an exciting re-creation of great scenes in history or of exotic foreign places. Giant painted canvases, hoisted onto rollers, would be slowly moved across the stage and as the scenes unfolded, the lecturer would relate to the enraptured crowds the dramatic sequence of events. One of the most popular subjects was "The Bombardment of Alexandria". Lights flashed on and off, drums rolled and crashed as the cannons of the British Fleet were seen to bombard the enemy's land batteries. A small orchestra provided stirring patriotic music as the drama unfolded, scene by scene, and the ships of the fleet moved ponderously across the stage.

The panorama of the nineteenth and early twentieth centuries was in a sense a predecessor to the cinema newsreel, allowing the public to experience great events that had been reported in the newspapers (for those who could read), but which required a good deal of imagination to visualise. Although appearing some months after the event, the public were nevertheless thrilled to witness

THE **SYNOD HALL,**
CASTLE TERRACE, EDINBURGH.

JOHN R. POOLE BY ARRANGEMENT WITH JURY'S IMPERIAL
PICTURES, LTD., PRESENTS

THE REX INGRAM PRODUCTION OF THE

**4 Horsemen ᵒᶠ ᵗʰᵉ Apocalypse**

TWICE DAILY    *Presented in every detail exactly as at the*
3 AND 8 P.M.    *Palace Theatre, Shaftesbury Avenue, London.*

**OFFICIAL PROGRAMME—PRICE 3d.**

the re-enactment of the defence of Rorke's Drift against the Zulu or the loss of the Titanic in frozen Atlantic seas.

It was Charles W. Poole who began to include Edinburgh regularly on his annual tour, bringing his panoramic Myriorama shows to the capital at Christmastime. Up to fifty subjects could be included in the programme with vaudeville acts, and later, short films brought in to fill the interval between tableaux. J.K.S. Poole describes the scene:

> "Poole's Myriorama, a series of large moving canvases and tableaux, was interspersed with variety acts which required the stage to be cleared and reset. A whistle was blown and a large linen graph sheet was pulled across the proscenium and pegged down, while a five- or six-minute Felix the Cat or single reel Chaplin short was screened. Meanwhile the stage was being prepared for acts — a conjuror, monocyclist, or equilibrist. The screen pulled off — on with the act — and at its conclusion another whistle, lights down, back with the screen with lights down and the stage being reset for the next tableau behind another short."

The popularity of the Myrioramas began to fade as more and more ambitious films came on to the screens. Charles's son, John R. Poole, entered the business with his father, leasing municipal halls he visited with the Myriorama to run "big pictures". In the decade after the First World War, *Scaramouche, The Four Horsemen of the Apocalypse* and other epics were seen at the Synod Hall. By the mid-twenties, films were being shown there continuously and the Myriorama performances had been reduced to one annual Christmas event. After almost a century, the touring days were finally over. The special affection that Edinburgh audiences held for the Myriorama encouraged its survival until 1928, well after any of its peers.

The family was now firmly committed to cinema entertainment. Jim Poole, just recently retired, and the third generation

Poole's Roxy by night, late 1940s

*The Scotsman*

Poole's Synod Hall in 1906 and in 1965, with J.K.S. Poole standing immediately to the left of the car in the lower picture.                           *J.K.S. Poole*

of the family to run the business, recalls that transition from live to big screen entertainment wasn't without hiccups.

"In the earlier film days, not knowing the Edinburgh climate sufficiently well, we were foolish enough to close the Synod Hall in the summer. I can remember staying at Gullane with my parents, and my father getting extremely angry at the weather — continuous rain and cold winds! We decided we wanted to return to our flat in Edinburgh, being sick and tired of the weather and more particularly — to the chagrin of my father — Mother and I were missing our weekly visit to St Andrew's Square Picture House with the added bonus of Sam and his Stage Band.

The following year the Synod Hall remained open during the summer — very successfully!"

In the next few years, expansion took place in Aberdeen, with the acquisition and conversion of the Palace Theatre into a supercinema and in 1932 the opening of the luxurious new Regent. Jim Poole was its first manager.

Continued success at the Synod Hall, now unfortunately the capital's famous "hole in the ground" behind the Usher Hall, encouraged further investment in the city's love for films. Poole's Roxy opened in 1937 and remains well loved in local memory for its successful and popular Mickey Mouse Club. In 1949, the former King's Cinema in the Tollcross district was re-opened by Pooles as the Cameo and over the next thirty-five years was to enjoy a reputation for quality cinema, hosting many of the Edinburgh Film Festival screenings. With its demise in 1982, the industry lost not only a fine cinema, but a long family tradition in entertainment.

## 2) KEMPS OF AYRSHIRE

By 1899, "President" Kemp's travelling cinema show "Dreamland" had joined the fast growing ranks of bioscope and cinematograph booths that were becoming a popular and exciting addition to the local fairs. With his son, Harry, the Leicester-born amusement proprietor toured two elaborate bioscope shows all over Britain in the decade after 1900, even taking the cumbersome outfit over to America and Canada for two seasons. When the cinema boom arrived, father and son were to choose the West of Scotland to launch a cinema-owning business that is still very much alive today. Encouraged by popular reaction to "Dreamland" at the annual Saltcoats fairs of previous years, the Kemps consolidated their business on the Ayrshire coast, taking their touring shows "off the road" for good in 1911 and opening their first cinema, the Pavilion, in Johnstone, Renfrewshire, later that year.

If Saltcoats folk are remembered as some of Scotland's most loyal cinema-goers, then it is to the Kemp family that they owe the distinction. Not content just to run the La Scala which they had built on a site in Hamilton Street in 1913, they erected a wooden building only yards away across the street which was run as a dance hall during the war, but was to open as the Casino cinema in 1919. As far as Saltcoats was concerned, cinema had arrived in force and young Harry, with a tradition of showmanship that was to delight local patrons for years to come, was to champion its cause.

With the popularity of films thus assured, Harry Kemp was eager to try out something new and had in mind to bring concert parties to the La Scala, designed to attract the annual holidaymaker to Ayrshire's premier summer resort. His father's initial doubts were dispelled when in 1922, the La Scala dropped pictures for six weeks and presented "Scottish Clans" with Dave Bruce as principal comedian. The show was an instant success and heralded a long and successful run of now legendary Kemp's Summer Shows at venues along the Ayrshire holiday coast. The

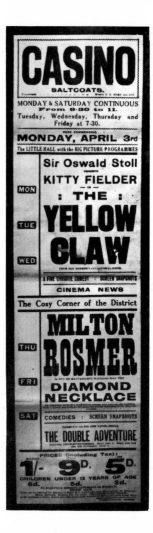

stars of these revues, Dave Willis, Renee and Billie Houston and Bobby Telford gained loyal local support in their subsequent careers in variety. Kemp's shows were toured far and wide to popular acclaim and helped many a stage career blossom.

Harry Kemp had taken full control of the family business on his father's retiral in 1925. The Pavilion, Johnstone, had been sold to the Glasgow-based Green family, but the circuit of picture houses was being enlarged. In 1930, the old wooden Casino was demolished and rebuilt as the plush new 1,200 seater Regal Cinema, opening the following year with the legionnaire adventure *Beau Ideal.* Seats were 3d (1½p) for the front stalls, rising to 9d (4p) for the circle. The third generation of Kemps, who would eventually take over the business, was that night just starting his career by selling chocolate to the patrons! With the De Luxe and later the Grange cinemas in Stevenston, the Kemp's name was foremost on the lips of anyone seeking entertainment in the district. Now under a fourth generation of family ownership, the Regal retains its reputation for high quality presentation and has one of the best 70mm systems in Scotland.

The cinemas were publicised very vigorously by Harry Kemp, adapting showman's traditions to attract patrons. Holidaymakers strolling along the esplanade and shoppers making their way home would find throw-aways thrust into their hands with all the details of the forthcoming features to be enjoyed at their local Kemp's cinema. Perhaps it was the close relationship to that other great fairground family, the Greens (Harry Kemp had married George Green's niece in 1908) that encouraged him to try films of local events called topicals. One of Green's advertising gags had been "Come and See Yourselves as Others See You", attracting audiences in the hope that they might spot themselves in a locally made film. It was a gimmick that many of the more enterprising independent exhibitors were to adopt for their own purposes.

Any local event which was well attended was a suitable topic. Cameramen would be instructed to get in as many faces as possible to maximise the potential audience when the film would be shown a few nights later. Harry Kemp had a considerable number

President Kemp's travelling bioscope show "Dreamland" attracting crowds at a local fair 1906.

The cast of the variety show at the Pavilion Cinema, Johnstone, welcomes Julian the Tank on a fund raising exercise c1917. President Kemp, wearing the bowler hat, is standing next to the nurse.

of these topicals made in the 1920s. Some he would shoot himself, not always confining the subject matter to parades or sports meetings. He was responsible for chronicling the disastrous flood which swept through Saltcoats' streets in the early 1920s, and had a film made of the triumphal return of the Ardrossan and Saltcoats Players with the prized Balasco Cup in 1928. The Nobel Explosives factory works' outing to Rothesay and the start of Saltcoats Pilgrimage to Lourdes were only two of the other local events to be relayed to delighted audiences. Shouts of ''There's wee Jeannie!'' and ''Is that you Wullie?'' echoed through the hall as familiar faces appeared in front of them, enlarged for all to see on the silver screen.

Obviously, any extra advert for the cinema was a bonus and, like many others of their ilk, these local films often included a shot of the cinema itself with staff posed in uniform on the vestibule steps. There is even one short fragment of film that has survived in the family's possession of Harry Kemp outside the Regal Cinema and, with the aid of new techniques of sound, bidding his patrons goodnight and a safe journey home. A truly flamboyant managerial style.

To the same Harry Kemp, however, belonged the unique distinction of making what must be one of the country's first party political broadcasts. In 1922, Mr. Kemp stood as a candidate for the local town council. Election day was approaching and unsuspecting patrons waiting for the start of the second feature must have been astonished to see before them on the screen — VOTE FOR HARRY KEMP. The film ran for one minute giving voters several reasons why they should choose Mr. Kemp as candidate and ending with a graphic illustration of how they should fill out the ballot paper the following Tuesday. It was nothing short of ingenious — and successful.

Ardrossan and Saltcoats players welcomed home in a topical film of 1928.

# 3) GREENS OF GLASGOW —
## "IF IT'S GOOD, IT'S GREEN'S"

By the 1890s, Glasgow's pre-eminent cinema family, the Greens, had already established with their fairground amusements a regular place in the city's entertainment at Christmas and during the Glasgow Fair holidays. It is to the proprietor of Green's Gallopers and Wiggle Woggle that many have attributed the first public performances of moving pictures in Scotland. Whether or not that is strictly true, George Green with his constant search for novelties for his carnival, must be credited with presenting some of the earliest regular film shows north of the border, at his site on the Old Barracks Carnival Ground in the city's Gallowgate.

Green's cinematograph booth with its handsomely ornate exterior was sparsely equipped inside. Fifty feet long and thirty feet broad, the admission was 1d (½p), rising to 2d (1p) when wooden forms were supplied for the 500 or so who could squeeze in. The programme lasted twenty minutes and would comprise several films each of less than a minute's duration. So lifelike were the flickering images that it was easy for the astonished audience to believe they were really happening. On one occasion during a screening of *Fingal's Cave* with the oncoming tide dashing against the rocks, a number of spectators backed out of the booth, unwilling "to stand there and get wet".

The mobile booths, costing as much as £6,000, were hauled round the country by large traction engines, which were used when stationary to generate electricity for the cinematograph performances. This produced a much brighter picture than was available to rural operators using "lime light" in village halls and converted shops. The fairground bioscopes eventually proved so popular that for their brief spell of supremacy it was not unknown for up to twenty booths to be showing films simultaneously at the same fair.

The Green family originated in Lancashire. Son of a master cabinet-maker, George Green rejected his father's trade to enter

Charlie Chaplin welcomes Fred Green onto the film set during one of several trips to the USA by the Glasgow film renter and exhibitor.

Green's travelling Cinematograph, one of the first to bring moving pictures to Scotland, c1896

Motor transportation used by Green's to distribute films to customers at the start of the First World War.

the world of entertainment. By 1890, he described himself as "travelling showman and proprietor of hobby horses" and his love of the fairground took him touring the length and breadth of the country. Although one of the first show families to settle down with permanent cinemas, he must have retained some affection for the nomadic life as in 1913 he bought from "President" Kemp (his niece's father-in-law) the beautiful bioscope show "Theatre Unique", which had replaced Kemp's "Dreamland" some years previously. Although by now the heyday of the fairground cinemas was past, nevertheless, George Green kept the "Theatre Unique" on the road until 1915, when it was brought to Glasgow, and its beautiful Marenghi organ placed in front of Green's first cinema in the Gallowgate, not far from the site of his earliest fairground shows.

The family entered the cinema business wholeheartedly. George Green, who died in 1915, had taken a bit of a gamble on the popularity of films back in 1902 when he acquired the Whitevale Theatre in the city's east end for the regular showing of films. With his two sons, Bert and Fred, who were to take over the business on his death, he carved out for the family a unique place in that small group of pioneers who were to give Scotland a longlasting and vigorous cinema industry. By the end of the First World War, the Greens had acquired or built some seven cinemas in the Glasgow area. The whole family helped out with the business. Indeed, for many years the Greens lived in a flat above the pay box of the Whitevale Theatre. Mrs. Green and three of her four daughters managed picture houses with friends and relatives, taking the money, selling sweets and keeping rowdy audiences under control. Bert and Fred kept up the momentum set by their father and did not restrict their activities purely to showing the films to an eager public whose demand was becoming difficult to meet.

To ensure a steady and reliable supply of films for their picture house, Green's Film Service was established in the years prior to 1914. From offices near Glasgow Cross, they organised a film renting and distribution network which served many of the exhibitors in the West of Scotland. They even had a go at producing story films for the screen, making a two-reel drama described as a farcical comedy in 1914. Audience reaction to the film is not recorded, but it may have had some influence on the failure to repeat the exercise! It did not, however, prevent them having another go at producing films which this time enjoyed modest success. Encouraged perhaps by the obvious attraction of their local topicals of earlier years, they began to produce cinema newsreels of Scottish events. Although production was hampered in the early days by the shortage of celluloid, the proudly-titled "Scottish Moving Picture News" began regular issues towards the end of the First World War. For the first time cinema audiences in Scotland could get coverage of local events side by side with the nationally produced Gaumont Graphic and Pathe Gazette newsreels that were becoming standard fare for cinema programmes. Encouraged by the success of this Scottish newsreel, ambitious plans for expansion were laid in 1919. The title of the newsreel was changed to "British Moving Picture News" and the legend "Green's Film Service, Glasgow and London" appeared on the credits. The first issue claimed to have "scooped" Asquith's wedding.

It is difficult to ascertain how long the newsreel survived into the 1920s as only a handful of the reels have escaped destruction. Certainly, it seems that they had long disappeared from the screens by the time Talkies arrived in force at the end of the decade.

The Greens were responsible for some of the earliest purpose-built cinemas in Scotland, a departure from the normal practice of taking over existing premises such as theatres or roller rinks for conversion to pictures. They were as ambitious in construction as they were in film production, using their own direct labour to build and furbish the new Picturedromes of the Greens' circuit. They even had their own printing company producing hand-bills, posters and programmes for publicity.

The pinnacle of achievement and their most enduring monument was the construction of two city centre super-cinemas in

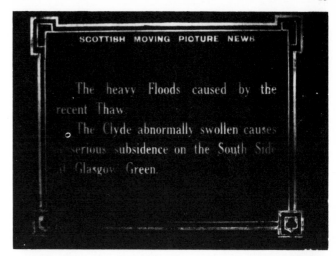

Glasgow and Dundee. With the opening of Green's Playhouse in Glasgow's Renfield Street in 1927, they had a city centre venue for the first time in the company's history and were all set to compete with rival circuits.

As a home for pictures the Playhouse broke new barriers. Catering for Glaswegians who were equally fond of dancing as well as picture-going, the building fulfilled a dual purpose. The massive auditorium seated 4,200 and had a full-sized orchestra pit to cater for the highest standard of musical accompaniment to silent films. Above the auditorium was a generous-sized ballroom, and with the vestibule tearooms, every facility was provided for eager patrons. In between auditorium and ballroom was a suite of offices from which the various administrative duties could be carried out. The design and size of the building was unique, claiming at the time to be the biggest cinema in Britain. The local Clerk of Works, however, had still to be convinced that the ballroom floor was strong enough to support a packed Saturday night dance crowd. Mr. Green responded by ordering his workmen to take six large cement mixers up to the ballroom and, by pushing them from side to side across the dance floor, silenced the Doubting Thomases.

Confident of the continued success of the industry, a second companion cinema, also named Playhouse, was erected on a prime site in Dundee's Nethergate. With only marginally fewer seats than its sister hall in Glasgow, the claim IF IT'S GOOD, IT'S GREEN'S woven into the cinema's carpeting exuded pride and confidence in the standard of entertainment offered to Dundonians.

Despite such an imposing presence within the industry in Scotland, the Green family business has proved less enduring than many of its contemporaries. All of Green's cinemas have been closed for some time, the Glasgow venue now popularly known as the Apollo Theatre, while the Dundee Playhouse hosts bingo. Even these two flagships in Glasgow and Dundee, although still standing, are in danger. The wavering fortunes of bingo, high rates and the premium on city centre sites make it unlikely that such cavernous and now difficult to fill venues will survive to testify to one family's contribution to an industry. As a rather sad footnote to such a glorious past, the company instructed all their records to be destroyed in 1980. That, coupled with the loss during the Second World War of most of their newsreels, leaves very little for historians to trace.

# 4) DONALD'S OF ABERDEEN, SINGLETON'S (WEST OF SCOTLAND CIRCUITS), AND THE ONSLAUGHT OF THE ODEONS

Entertainers and showmen may have dominated the cinema business in its early years, but not all the family concerns in Scotland had their origins in touring. Whereas the show-families had inherited a tradition of entertainment and a feeling for the bustle of the crowd, other family businesses were also to make their mark on the trade. Without the same personal attachment to the fairground world of their rivals, they perhaps tended to regard the new craze for "movies" in a slightly more business-like manner. Nevertheless, their contribution to the industry was just as important and, in its own way, equally durable.

Aberdeen's uniquely successful Donald circuit was founded about the time of the First World War by James F. Donald. He had a bicycle shop in the city and was running a small dancing Academy when he opened his first cinema in the West End. Occupying a hall above dairy premises in Union Street, it quickly earned the nickname "tuppenny freezer". Like the Greens in Glasgow, the whole of James Donald's family helped out in the fledgling business and in the 1920s, he moved to new premises opening the Grand Central in George Street and established a long-running tradition in the city's cinema history.

For the next twenty years, Donald's were locked in competition with rival circuit Aberdeen Picture Palaces, run by pioneer Bert Gates, whose Capitol cinema, opened in 1933, gave Aberdeen a picture theatre to match the best in the country. It is one of the few cinemas to retain its cinema organ in working order. The Donalds finally won the battle for cinema supremacy in 1941 when Aberdeen Picture Palaces accepted their offer and relinquished control of the circuit to their rivals. Only three cinemas in the city had not fallen under the Donalds' sway: the Picture House and Poole's two halls, the Regent and the Palace.

Capitol Cinema, Aberdeen

*K.S. Wheelan*

Capitol, Aberdeen, interior                    *K.S. Wheelan*

For the preceding five years, the big circuits had been trying to get a foothold in the city as the trend to enlarge and consolidate cinema outlets grew in strength. Both Gaumont-British and ABC had been unsuccessful in their attempts to absorb the smaller companies, although County Cinemas had managed to take over Poole's interest in their two cinemas. Unable to buy into existing companies, ABC began construction of a new super cinema of its own on a site in the Shiprow. The war delayed construction and it was eventually to take another decade to complete the building, which opened as the Regal in 1954.

Meanwhile, ABC's great national rivals, the Gaumont-British circuit, owned by J. Arthur Rank, had squeezed in through County Cinemas, which Rank in turn had taken over in 1939. With the later addition of the Oscar Deutsch chain of cinemas, this massive conglomerate was to make its first impact upon Aberdeen by re-naming the Regent, along with other cinemas acquired in this period, as the Odeon.

Odeons had already appeared north of the Border, mostly in the Glasgow area, and largely due to the activities of just one family concern led by George Singleton. As a boy of eight or nine, he recalls his first experience of moving pictures.

"There was a bill poster named Mr George who, greatly daring, started to run cinemas on his own. He took the Town Hall, Clydebank, for a Saturday night, and he paid my father to play the piano. Now, of course, it was a very different thing then from the cinemas we've got to know now, because films were short, seven or eight minutes, maybe ten minutes. A projector was set up at one end and a screen tied up at the other and the people sat in between. There was only one projector, so there was an interval between each reel, and sometimes to fill in the gaps they put on an illustrated singer, with slides illustrating the song. I can remember very well, quite vividly, and you know it must be eighty years ago, sitting on

the platform at the Town Hall, Clydebank, my
father playing away.''

These Saturday night shows presented by James George were
subsequently recalled as some of the finest in the country and
much credit was given to the first-class accompaniment provided by pianist Richard Singleton. He had been running a printing
business producing handbills, tickets, and publicity material for
concerts and variety shows, and this involvement in the entertainment industry and his own love of music encouraged him to
start up on his own in the cinema. He began cautiously by running a series of one night stands in municipal halls in several
Lanarkshire towns. In March 1910, he opened his first regular
cinema by taking a lease on the former Masonic Hall at Burnbank in Hamilton. Spartanly equipped, with a corrugated tin box
for the projector at the back and wooden forms for the patrons,
it was attended regularly by local miners, who chose to squat
along the walls ''on their hunkers''. Young George Singleton,
proud of the fact that he could do every job in the cinema in
those days, helped his father run the picture shows, selling
toffees and caramels, taking tickets, and on one occasion,
standing in for the pianist.

"I remember one night the pianist didn't turn up
and I had to learn three tunes and I had to play
them right through the night, one after the
other.''

Armed with this expertise, George was ready to strike out
on his own, his first venture being partnership in a former United
Free Church in Glasgow's Gorbals, the optimistically named
''Paragon'', making full use of the original church pews to
squeeze in as many people as possible. By 1924 George Singleton,
in his own words ''had two Empires — Napoleon had nothing
on me!'', both Empires being former music halls in Coatbridge
and Dundee. The steady expansion of the family holdings saw
Singleton cinemas reaching their peak in 1935 with fourteen halls
spread throughout Scotland.

''Mr. Cosmo'', the symbol of Singleton's city centre cinema in Glasgow.

The Vogue Cinema, Govan, 1938

By now, the organisation headed by Oscar Deutsch was beginning to seriously challenge the major circuits down south. Although best remembered for the distinctive style of Odeon architecture he masterminded, Deutsch's company were now looking beyond building their own cinemas to expansion and acquisition of existing cinemas in their efforts to build up a national circuit.

In 1937, his busiest year, Oscar Deutsch took over two other circuits, one in the Home Counties and the other the Singleton group in Scotland. Along with the former church in the Gorbals, still equipped with its wooden pews, and an old mission hall in Falkirk, Deutsch acquired some eight other cinemas, renaming most of them Odeon and very quickly establishing a presence from Hawick to Dundee. If George Singleton had rapidly acquired two Empires by the time he was twenty-four, he had equally quickly disposed of them a dozen years later!

Undaunted by the dramatic turn of events, George Singleton set out afresh. The second time around, he was able to start off on a much grander scale. When the first Vogue opened in Govan in July 1938, it was a far cry from the days of old church pews and penny admissions. Contemporary accounts described the new cinema as a superior picture house, with bright and attractive neon lighting. In all, quite a luxury for Govanites, whose appetite for films seemed insatiable.

The name "Vogue" was chosen to symbolise the new chain of Singleton cinemas which were to serve Glasgow's suburbs for the remainder of their cinema days. Apart from the speciality city-centre Cosmo (now the Glasgow Film Theatre), none of these theatres still shows films. The tradition of providing the entertainment that the public wants still runs strongly in the family, however, with most of the buildings surviving almost intact hosting bingo sessions, and perhaps just waiting quietly for the next "Vogue" in public entertainment to materialise.

# 5) ABC'S SCOTTISH ORIGINS, FILM RENTING, AND A.B. KING'S C.A.C.

The early ventures of the show-families into cinema management had not gone unnoticed by the financiers and businessmen of the Edwardian era. Encouraged by new regulations laid down by the 1909 Cinematograph Act and aware of the rising tide of respectability that cinema was beginning to enjoy, several groups of city businessmen and professionals began to enter the industry. Investments of this kind were almost always of a purely commercial nature, obscured behind company names and leaving the promotion and publicity with which audiences were beginning to associate film-going to the managers employed to supervise the various cinemas in their corporate control.

One of the most outstanding success stories of this kind of exhibiting has its origins most decidedly in Scotland. Who would have guessed that when John Maxwell, senior partner in the Glasgow law firm of Maxwell, Hodgson & Co. incorporated a small company under the name of Scottish Cine and Variety Theatres in 1916, that it would eventually become a household name, synonymous with cinema in the UK? As Associated British Cinemas (ABC), it was to have a glittering future.

However, in 1916, Maxwell's tidy legal mind was thinking along much smaller lines. By linking his interests in cinemas with those of his new partners, James Wright and Jimmy Milne, he was creating a small group of cinemas that would have more bargaining power with the renters of the day. His partners both went on to create a name for themselves in exhibiting in Scotland, but it is with John Maxwell's name that the subsequent rapid expansion of the circuit is traditionally linked.

By the mid-1920s, the circuit had grown considerably. David A. Stewart a variety agent who had joined Maxwell early in the Company's life, was given the task of running the new subsidiary, Kirkcaldy Entertainments Company. The Fife town had five cinemas all of which now fell to Scottish Cine and Variety Theatres. It was an astute move on Maxwell's part as Kirkcaldy, with at that time more cinemas per head of population than any town in Scotland, was a prime target.

The circuit went from strength to strength, expanding its interests south of the Border. In a story now firmly embedded in the history of the cinema in Britain, John Maxwell's leadership created in 1928 ABC, later the Associated British Picture Corporation. Merged with its Scottish sister company in 1932, ABC began to emerge as the single biggest rival to Gaumont British (themselves to be swallowed up later with the Odeon group into the Rank empire). By 1941, the two rivals had firmly laid claim to their territories. Ironically in that same year, John Maxwell and his counterpart in the opposite camp, Oscar Deutsch, both died.

The success of cinema-owning depended very largely on getting the best films. A good supply of popular films was an absolute prerequisite and here, as in many other areas, John Maxwell's company was to lead the field. By the early 1930s, he had brought under his control not only an impressive circuit of cinemas in most of the major towns in Britain, but had acquired the means of producing and distributing the films to these outlets. With British International Pictures' studios at Elstree, control of renting company Wardour Films, and distribution controlled by Pathe and the American First National Company, he created the first camera-to-screen combination in the history of the industry, ensuring for his cinemas a steady supply of product and for the studios a guaranteed outlet for their films.

Celluloid was the vital fuel of the cinema from its inception in the early days of smoky booths, flickering images and cricked necks. At first, the films were bought outright by anyone who wanted them. The films were sold at a fixed price of 4d. (1½p) a foot, most of the reels in those days being less than 1,000ft. long. As the programme would be made up of a number of short films, the purchase price was quite steep, often greater than the takings for the show. The public expected two different programmes a week and for the exhibitor with only one hall, it could be difficult to make a profit. The situation was eased with the

One of ABC's first cinemas, the Govan, Glasgow 1930.

The Port Brae Cinema, Kirkcaldy 1930.

appearance of the renter, a middleman between the makers and the exhibitors. The renter would buy the film from the producers and rent to the exhibitor for three days. The price for the first run was set higher than for the following three-day hire and so on down the line, the smaller halls getting the films at the cheapest rate, but quite some time after their release. George Singleton recalls going in to the renter's office as a boy to book films for his father's cinema at 7/6d. (37½p) a reel — by that time the film was three months old! During their three day hire, the exhibitor could do what he liked with the film, running it in more than one cinema on the same night if it could be arranged. George frequently ran between his father's two cinemas in Blantyre and Burnbank with the next reel of film in the programme.

"Indeed my father bought his first motor car because the Chaplin films came out and they were so popular we wanted to run them in more than two cinemas on the same night, and he bought his first motor car so that he could do this."

The popularity of the new film stars like Charlie Chaplin and Mary Pickford created their own problems for the renters. Everybody wanted the film's first run and to satisfy demand, the renters had to buy multiple copies. Cinemas were saturated with the films, and the renters, unable to recoup their outlay, faced financial difficulties. The solution for some was to be found in the "exclusive" film. Under this new system, the renter released the film to only one cinema to the exclusion of any other venue within a certain radius. This exhibitor made money on the film and was thus able to pay a higher rental for it. It would be released to other cinemas in the area when the first exhibitor had finished his run.

The exclusive system squeezed out the old open market method and by 1914 had established itself throughout the country. The war came and with it the closure of nearly all the European film studios. American films flooded the market and, anxious to ensure a guaranteed supply of films, exhibitors entered into block bookings on an exclusive basis for one and sometimes as much as two years ahead. There were sacrifices to this new efficiency in the industry. The small independent local renters, who had served their immediate area so well in previous years, now faced competition on a scale they were unable to beat. The big producing companies began opening provincial offices to rent their own films direct to the exhibitors. The independents might manage to pick up a local agency if they were lucky, but by 1918 most of the pioneers of renting had disappeared from the scene.

In the heyday of the cinema before the Second World War there were as many as twenty different renters with offices in Scotland. The big names like Gaumont, Pathe, RKO, and Paramount all had a city centre office. They would run trade shows, previews of new films to which exhibitors would be invited and then the salesmen would call on them to negotiate the best possible price. Although by the late 1930s the big circuits like ABC and Gaumont-British could book for several hundred cinemas at a time, there were still a great number of independents and smaller groups of cinemas looking for product for their screens. In many cases they would engage a booking agent to act on their behalf and with a number of screens at his disposal, the agent was in a better position to negotiate with the renters.

The outstanding figure in this territory was Sir Alexander B. King, remembered by his colleagues in the trade for championing the exhibitors' cause against the iniquitous Entertainments Tax, introduced in 1916. A.B. King is given much of the credit for achieving the reduction of the tax on cheaper seats, thus relieving the smaller exhibitor of some of the financial burden. A.B. King continued to press for abolition of the tax through the Cinematograph Films Council and the owners' own organisation, the Cinematograph Exhibitors Association. His own career began in Glasgow at the age of twelve, as a programme seller in the Princess Theatre in the Gorbals, collecting used programmes from under the seats, ironing them out and re-selling them at a later performance! Subsequently manager of the Lorne Cinema in the city in 1914, he worked steadily throughout the 1920s becoming a director of some ninety cinemas by the time of his knighthood

Playhouse Cinema, Elgin.

Sir A. B. King,

in 1944. He was the principal booking manager for Caledonian Associated Cinemas, an Inverness-based Scottish company, whose humble beginnings with nine cinemas in the north-east in 1935 had risen to forty-nine some fifteen years later.

The most serious rival to ABC in Scotland, Caley's hold on the northern half of the country provided a solid base from which to expand, buying up cinemas in the Lothians and Fife. With all these outlets behind him, Sir A.B. King commanded respect from the renters, whose visits to his office rarely went according to their pre-conceived strategy. He was a master at negotiating bookings and could generally get the better of the salesmen. A universally liked and respected figure, he contributed much to the status of the cinema in Scotland during his lifetime and was admired by colleagues in the industry both at home and in the American heartland of the movies.

# PART 3. CINEMA STAFF

## 1) MANAGERS — J.S. NAIRN

Looking back over the history of cinema in Scotland, it would be difficult to deny that owning picture houses was in general a fairly profitable business. Whatever motivated the early entrepreneurs to gamble on the success of moving pictures, their courage paid off handsomely in the decades to follow.

If the trade was good to the exhibitors, however, it did not necessarily follow that those who literally "exhibited" the pictures were to benefit in the same way. For years the projectionists, usherettes and managers who staffed the picture palaces and the "bug huts" worked under conditions and wages that few of their contemporaries would have tolerated outside. One projectionist recalls being taken on by a certain exhibitor whose employees could be dismissed at one minute's notice. This must be taken as an unusually extreme case, but it was certainly true that working conditions were not good: long anti-social hours, low wages and little security of tenure. In considering why the staff put up with these conditions, it must be said that they were slow to organise and form a union. In times of unemployment, jobs were sought after at any price and it was an employers' market. However, these factors applied to other workplaces too.

Picture house employees had one major disadvantage in dealing with their employers. In general, they were attracted to the cinema and to the excitement it seemed to offer. There was, for many, a personal commitment to films that compensated for the disadvantages of working in the industry. Many started straight from school, being brought up on the Saturday matinees and the regular family outing to the pictures. The lure of the silver screen, the excitement of starting up the projectors and what they saw as the glamour of the industry in many cases blinkered their appreciation of the reality of their working situation.

The hours were long (an average 60 hour week was not uncommon) and were usually worked when most other people were at leisure. The anti-social nature of the job meant that for many cinema staff, their only associates were other cinema employees,

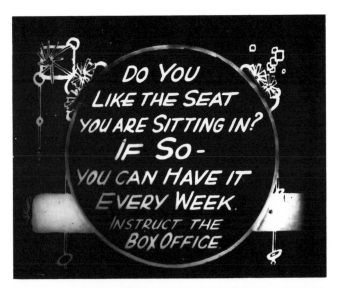

Facilities offered to regular patrons at the cinema.

who were off duty at the same time of day. It was perhaps more difficult for managers and projectionists, who were frequently transferred from cinema to cinema to gain experience and could find themselves in a different town or right across the other side of the city away from their friends and family. The staffs of cinemas in close proximity to each other could become very friendly and would often arrange to go out together when their days off coincided, perhaps after the cinema closed, to go as a group to a dance hall.

With relatively little social contact outwith the industry, it was difficult for the individual to compare his or her lot with contemporaries in other trades. It was noticeable, for example, how many projectionists took a less enthusiastic view of their profession on returning from military service in the Second World War. Many recall how the taste of a different way of life had made them realise how much they had missed in their youth through long hours spent shut off in the projection box.

The manager was the kingpin in the employee hierarchy. His was a skilled public relations exercise and as the member of staff who had most contact with the public, it was his attitude that set the tone of the cinema itself. The good manager was always to be seen smartly dressed, standing at front-of-house at the start of each performance. Patrons could rely on him for an opinion on the films to be seen and for courteous attention to their complaints. He would acknowledge the regulars, who would not hesitate to call him if someone was sitting in "their seat". He was required to be tactful at all times — a quality particularly useful when a big picture was held over for an extra week and he would have to explain to regular patrons why their established ritual of Monday night at the pictures was upset.

Of all the tasks in the cinema, the manager's was perhaps the least regimented. Apart from having to cope with everything from floods in the toilets, to lost children and patrons fainting, there was scope for individual flair and enthusiasm generally denied the auditorium and projection staff. If there is one man who demonstrated that potential fully throughout his long career in the cinema, it was James S. Nairn, cinema manager for some fifty years. There were managers like him all over the country who built up a local reputation for always doing something different to publicise a new film and raise a laugh. Relating Jimmy Nairn's achievements pays tribute to them all.

Young Jimmy was serving his apprenticeship in Harland and Wolff's shipyard in Glasgow when he first began to take an interest in the cinema. He took a weekend job as operator at the film shows run by Scottish Cine and Variety Theatres in the local burgh hall and by 1917, was chief projectionist in the Govan Cinema, one of the first of John Maxwell's circuit-to-be. He was a born showman and his love of the industry and his diligence earned swift promotion. As a young man of twenty-four, he was offered the job of manager of the Savoy, Edinburgh. Jimmy recalls his reaction:

> "Immediately my vision went to the Savoy, Glasgow, which was a big super colossal and I wondered how on earth, with no experience at all, at the age of twenty-four, how I would manage to do this. However, I met the Managing Director and we went through to Edinburgh and he took me down to Stockbridge and showed me the Savoy and my heart sank. It wasn't a big super colossal, it was an old shooting range converted to a cinema with 906 seats and a three piece 'orchestra'; a cello, a violin and piano."

Whether or not it was intentional, the company had found themselves an enterprising manager who now brought all his youthful enthusiasm to bear on what had become a rather complacently run, slightly neglected cinema. It was a small dingy hall, whose former monopoly in the district had induced a lethargic attitude to publicity and management. Jimmy did what he could to bring back the patrons, but was hampered early on in his efforts by lack of co-operation from head office. He had ideas for a series of local topicals — the classic "Come and See Yourselves" idea which was working so well elsewhere, but the

Jimmy Nairn and wife Mary with colleagues in the trade welcoming film star Jameson Thomas to the 1929 Edinburgh Cinema Ball. (Note the Chaplin-style moustache on Jimmy Nairn.)

38

The Playhouse, Inverness, decorated for the northern premiere of "IVANHOE" 1952.

The newly opened Ritz Cinema, Edinburgh, showing "BLACKMAIL", one of the first British "Talkies".

company refused to put up the money for film stock. (In fact, none of the major circuits, except CAC, ever did go into their own local newsreels; it was very much the independents' gimmick). Not to be deterred, Jimmy went round the local shopkeepers and by promising to include a shot of their shopfronts, raised the necessary cash to start up his series "The Savoy presents". A whole run of topicals followed and as the scheme progressed, the "Where to Shop in Stockbridge" issues provided both entertainment for patrons in looking out for friends and neighbours and useful advertising for local businesses.

Jimmy was developing an interest in making films as well as showing them and had built much of the equipment he needed to process and title the films himself. His success was noted at head office and early in 1929 he was offered promotion as manager of a brand new cinema to be built in Edinburgh that year. The Ritz was more like the picture palace he had envisaged some five years previously. A site had been acquired in Rodney Street and plans were almost completed. Jimmy embarked almost right away on an ambitious scheme to film the construction of the cinema from start to finish. At regular intervals over the ensuing months, he would be seen on the site with unwieldy 35mm camera and tripod, shooting another stage in the construction process. People were to remark later when the film was completed that never had they seen carpenters and brick-layers work so fast. Jimmy wryly explained that as soon as they saw him with his camera they worked like fury, knowing that their bosses were likely to see the film later on!

The cinema was publicised as one of the first to be built for sound, only achieving that distinction as its design has been altered mid-way through construction to make room for the new Talkie apparatus. The doors were opened on 10th September, 1929, with Al Jolson in *The Singing Fool*. Patrons marvelling at the phenomenon of "Talkies" were allowed a rare peep behind the scenes when Jimmy's film of the construction of the Ritz was shown during the first week. As a finale he had taken the camera up to the projection box and had filmed the sound discs and projectors as they were running. All the staff were posed one by one for the camera and even the cleaners were portrayed hoovering the plush new tip-up seats. It was a roaring success.

Regular patrons of the Ritz, like those of the Savoy before them, came to anticipate something different from Jimmy Nairn. He used a great deal of imagination and inventiveness in decorating the foyer of the cinema and its showcase window facing the street to reflect the theme of a film. He was to take all these ideas with him and develop them further during his next spell, at the Regal in Stirling. Transferred there in 1934, he was to widen the role of the cinema within the community.

During the town's annual Infirmary Week in aid of local charities, Jimmy organised and presented the Regal's Midnight Show, commencing on a Friday after the last film performance. Each year, the show was a resounding success, giving local stars a chance to perform and all in aid of charity. The annual parade of decorated floats on Charities Day was filmed by Jimmy for the Regal and he personally contributed a great deal of time and energy to fund-raising and community life. It was with great regret that he had to announce to his many friends in the summer of 1941 that he was leaving Stirling to take up a new appointment. It was to be a break with the company that he had loyally served for over twenty-five years.

The new post was to take him north to Inverness to manage the Playhouse cinema and to supervise two other picture houses, the La Scala and the Empire. All were owned by Caledonian Associated Cinemas and it was with this organisation that he was to remain for the rest of his life. Although he was later to be promoted to Controller of the Northern Area of CAC, his first love was for front-of-house contact he had as manager with patrons. Inverness cinema-goers were to get to know and love Jimmy for his imaginative and affectionate management.

He had a soft spot for children and every Christmas would painstakingly decorate the foyer and tearoom in the Playhouse as a Christmas fairyland to which generations of children will remember being taken as an annual treat. After the disastrous

The Regal Cinema, Stirling, in the 1930s.

"CENTRAL AIRPORT"

An elaborate set for "CENTRAL AIRPORT", a First National picture of 1933, recreated by Jimmy Nairn with the use of painted backcloths, papier mâché hills and model people and aircraft. The pièce de résistance was the ingenious concoction of a continuous band upon which were fixed a number of model aeroplanes. These were seen to be flying over the airport tarmac. The whole apparatus was constructed from a bicycle wheel, a wooden roller and some gramophone needles.

Jimmy Nairn at the Burleta organ.

"Maybe once a month I came away with a stage turn to fool the audience and this particular one was an organ. The reason why I chose an organ was that all the super cinemas in Edinburgh were moving in to organs. So I built a replica of an organ, three keyboards and used 78 rpm gramophone records as the music which the organist was supposed to play. The name of the organ was Burleta, which I looked up in Italian meant "fake", but nobody twigged that, they just thought it was the name of the organ. Now so that I couldn't be accused of false pretences, I put a little boy inside the organ and when it was moved off the stage, the audience saw the little boy inside with a pair of household bellows pumping away. But nobody laughed. I thought that would create a great laugh. They were quite convinced it was a real organ. As a matter of fact, an organist from one of the churches had written to my head office at that time asking to see this organ being built, because I'd covered it up a wee bit the week before. And, of course, I got into trouble from the head office for buying a four thousand pound organ through my petty cash!"

fire which destroyed the Playhouse in 1974, he turned his own home into a wonderland at Christmastime, so that the children would not be disappointed. The Playhouse, under his direction, had become a focal point for many Inverness families, who spent many happy evenings in front of the silver screen.

It wasn't necessary to perform publicity stunts to be a good cinema manager, although it tended to lift the image of the picture house and boost attendances. For those short of imagination, there were always suggestions in the printed Campaign Books that renters provided with each film. For *Mr Deeds Goes to Town*, an early Gary Cooper picture, Columbia offered for hire a Stars and Stripes suit for any employee who could be persuaded to parade up and down the streets in it. Some of the circuits offered prizes for the best exploitation gimmick of the month and there were various trade awards to aim for. It was up to the individual manager, and some entered into it with more gusto than others. Ken Smith, a manager in the Rank circuit, even persuaded his wife to dress up as Carmen Miranda for *On the Road to Rio*. The managers' enthusiasm for such gimmicks didn't always carry down to their staff. Charlie Hamill remembers the manager of the Paragon in the Gorbals trying to persuade all his attendants to wear straw boaters and glasses for the Harold Lloyd picture that was playing. Only one man, the doorman, could be encouraged to do it.

Doormen or Commissionaires in the grander halls of the 1920s, were often ex-servicemen, their military bearing and imposing uniform helping to create an authoritarian impression, particularly useful in dealing with a restless queue for the Saturday matinee. In the super cinemas with several thousand seats, the Commissionaires would be in charge of a corps of page-boys in little pill-box hats, who directed patrons to the cloakroom or the tearooms as required. These page-boys were often governed by a rod of iron as tough military discipline would be brought to bear and a rigorous inspection of brass buttons and finger-nails conducted prior to opening for the first house. The Commissionaire was the butt of many a ribald comment from the queues for the one and nines, but he was always obeyed as he could wield the ultimate in deterrents. He could stop you getting in! The doorman, or in the early days of penny gaffs, often the exhibitor himself, could ruin a youngster's week. One particular exhibitor from those early years is remembered by David Gouk for his ruthless methods.

"On Saturdays he would line up all the children and would say 'Sorry, Willie, sorry, but ye canna come in today. Sorry Geordie, ye canna come in.' And they'd say 'Why, Mr. Scott?' And he would say 'Because you're too fat!' He wouldn't let them in until last because it was all forms and he squeezed them in twenty to a form at a penny (½p) a time."

## 2) AUDITORIUM STAFF —
## ATTENDANTS AND MUSIC MAKERS

"The attendants who show people to their seats can help you to make friends or they can drive trade away." With these pearls of wisdom the *Kinematograph Weekly's* "How to Run a Picture Theatre" opens its section on auditorium staff. For the super cinemas of the 1930s, lavishly furbished and priding themselves on first class entertainment it was important that the staff lived up to the image of the theatre. They were expected to maintain the highest standards and were governed, at least in Bessie Fury's experience, by a strict code of conduct and by almost military standards of dress. As one of a complement of twelve usherettes at the newly opened Regal in Glasgow's Sauchiehall Street, Bessie recalls the daily routine.

"First of all we had a parade every day. We had tunics with brass buttons and the skirts and the big Spanish hats. It was a beautiful uniform and, of course, black silk stockings and black shoes. These had all to be polished and everything had to be perfect. Mr. Morrison, the manager, came down and he would inspect us all. He was awfully nice but very, very strict. If there was a wrinkle in your stocking that was it, 'Up and get that fixed'."

Parade was at 12.30pm and the doors opened to the public about 1.00pm. "You went on duty and you each stood at a gangway and as you filled it up, you passed the people on with your torch to the next gangway. And you weren't allowed to speak and you weren't allowed to sit down. You stood all the time."

It was a long day. After about two hours, there was a tea break — "minutes" as they were called by the staff — when there was a chance for a cup of tea and a few minutes' seat.

"Of course, we were terribly busy, you never got a minute. You'd an hour for tea, but if, Satur-

Attendants at the Regal, Glasgow, at its opening in 1929.

day especially, you were terribly busy you were allowed up for a cup of tea and then back on duty. We worked Christmas Day and New Year's Day. For all that, you'd never get any extra money. It was just taken for granted.''

On most nights the programme finished about 10.30pm. The usherettes had been standing on duty for an average ten hours, not allowed to talk to each other and with very little time to relax. It was a six-day working week and with a basic wage of £1.2.6d. (£1.12½p) it was not surprising that some of the girls had to take the opportunity to earn a little extra by working the trade shows that were held at the Regal at ten in the morning. But despite the long hours and strict regime, Bessie enjoyed her years in the cinema, recalling that at the time she was lucky to be in a job. She was proud of the fact that when she was there, the Regal was *the* cinema in town.

The Regal usherettes' long days were enlivened by the musical interlude that by the 1930s had become standard fare for city centre cinemas. The Compton and Wurlitzer organs were a feature of the grander halls and the organists became minor stars in their own right. Richard Telfer, resident organist at the Rutland and later New Victoria cinemas in Edinburgh, remembers the great gusto with which patrons would join in the community singing in the interval entertainment. The organist had to exercise his own judgement in choosing the tone of the music for these interludes. (Audiences for ''intellectual'' pictures were not renowned for their community singing.) As nine out of ten films appealed to the popular market, however, these sing-a-longs were more often than not part of the regular programme of music.

Organs first appeared in the silent era, replacing the full-scale orchestras in the big picture houses. With complex sound effects facilities, they were flexible and economical aids to the programme. In the early days, two organists would work shifts to split the day's programme and as Talkies came in, they found themselves required to sit at the console for most of the programme ready to strike up a chord whenever the film broke down.

As the Talkie apparatus improved and there were fewer mishaps, there was less need for instantaneous musical fillers and the number of musicians was reduced to leave a solo organist for the interval period.

Much has been said about the wholesale redundancies of musicians with the introduction of Talkies in the early 1930s. However, many exhibitors had scant sympathy for them as their constant demands for higher wages had pushed overheads up enormously. It was often more expensive to pay the orchestra than to hire the films. Most, being professional musicians, regarded their evenings in the cinemas as an extra, many having day-to-day jobs playing in tea salons and coffee houses or teaching music. Nevertheless, their disappearance was mourned by many members of the public, who as music lovers, often went to a particular cinema to listen to the orchestra rather than to see the film.

A full size orchestra was rarely found outside the ''supers''. For the majority of the smaller suburban halls, a musical trio was adequate, a pianist at the very least. Agnes Taylor began playing piano accompaniment for films in 1912 at the age of eighteen. The leader of her little ''orchestra'' was a professional violinist, who brought with him the music for the cello, drums, cornet and piano that made up the ensemble.

''Saturday was a very long day because you played the Saturday matinee on your own. The band came in at half past six and they played until half past ten and then they packed up. They'd no soul for the picture — anybody could be dying or saying their last words or something like that on the screen. 10.30pm. Violins clicked in the box and away they went. You were left there to hold the fort. Sometimes, the last of the queue weren't in till after 9 o'clock so it would be after 11.00pm before I went home.''

It was the pianist who had the responsibility for watching the screen and signalling to the rest of the ensemble when a change of mood took place. Occasionally, the renters would provide

Allan Kennedy, resident organist at the Regal, Glasgow.

musical cue sheets to help the accompanist, but in many of the smaller cinemas, the pianists had to develop skills of improvisation, which weren't always appreciated by the audiences especially when they were desperately trying to cover for a breakdown in the film. Tempting as it must have been, they were warned, "Don't chip in with 'Oh Dear, What Can The Matter Be?' — that old joke has got too hoary and it may mean a week's notice for you." (Kine Weekly: *Playing to Pictures.*)

In the history of the cinema, it is these musicians who are usually portrayed as sacrificial lambs on the altar of the talking pictures. They didn't have exclusive rights to this dubious distinction, however. Probably largely forgotten by historians of the industry were the lowliest of the cinema staff — the chocolate sellers. Their task wasn't so easy as it is today, for without an interval devoted exclusively to advertising and selling confectionery, the chocolate boy had to conduct his business during the actual film show itself. He needed a strong voice to carry over the strains of the band down at the front and the arguments between patrons in the stalls swapping theories on how the goodie, out-numbered by his foes, was going to overcome the opposition and rescue the girl!

The chocolate seller, parading up and down the aisles during the films, must have felt some despair at the coming of Talkies. At first, it wasn't too bad, the early sound films still having silent bits where a stentorian "Chocolates! Caramels!" could still be heard in the ninepennies. But with the All Talking, All Singing Picture, the task became more difficult. As Charlie Hamill explained, it wasn't just the love of the job that spurred the chocolate boys on to greater efforts.

"I was fourteen and still at school. I started by selling chocolates in the evenings at a place called the Paragon in the Gorbals. You worked a commission. We got three shillings in the pound. My wage actually worked out at an average of about twelve shillings (60p) a week. A bar of chocolate cost tuppence (1p)."

In fact, Charlie Hamill's sales were so good that when he was subsequently offered a full-time job as apprentice projectionist, he was faced with a problem.

"The rate for a spool boy was only ten shillings (50p) a week, so it meant that I'd to take a reduction. So, they gave me the wage I was getting selling chocolate."

### 3) PROJECTIONISTS — "IN THE BOX."

The average cinema-goer probably rarely stopped to think what was going on behind the small square window high up in the back wall of the auditorium. As long as the flickering shaft of light streamed over their heads and produced a larger than life image on the screen, they were well content. Only if something went wrong would they acknowledge that such a person as projectionist existed. Unlike today, the audiences, especially the children, would shout and stamp their feet until the fault was corrected. Katie Smith recalls the penny matinee at the "Starry" in Edinburgh.

"The picture would come on. You'd just see the feet and we'd say 'Down a bit, down a bit, up a bit, along a bit!', and we're shouting at the operator and going on like this, and people were sitting at the side and they used to get annoyed, and there was a ledge where these windows were covered with tin and they used to bang at this tin and then — silence! The picture would come right."

The projectionists were shut off from the auditorium for the duration of the day's programme. In many ways they were distant from the public side of cinema life and this was reflected in their position within the staff. While the manager concerned himself with the daily routine and the behaviour of the auditorium and front-of-house staff, he could usually leave the technical side in the capable hands of the chief projectionist and his assistants.

Many a "chief" began in his teens as a spool boy, or apprentice. The standard rate of pay for these youngsters for many years was ten shillings (50p) a week and for that they had to put in long hours. An average of 55-60 hours per week was not uncommon, and that didn't allow for overtime or late-running shows.

The spool boy's duties were to rewind the reels of film, to repair joins, and thread up the next reel ready for projection.

A regular announcement in the early days of touring cinemas when there was only one projector in use.

He would also be required to change the carbon rods in the arc lamps, an important task having a direct bearing on the continued brightness of the picture on the screen, and perform countless small jobs for his "chief". It was also the task of the spool boy to collect and return the reels of film to the renter's offices or local film depot after the show. Most cinemas changed their programmes twice weekly and as Johnny Mulhearn recalls, for the spool boy it was an onerous task to be performed over and above the daily routine.

"Every Wednesday night and every Saturday night after the show, you'd to go round all the film renters delivering your films and it would be about midnight. And the same thing on a Monday morning and Thursday morning. You'd to go away with your suitcase and collect the films and carry them all back again!"

Because of the inflammable nature of the old cinema films, the spool boys weren't allowed on the tramcars. David Gouk recalls that they would try all sorts of dodges to escape the vigilant eye of the conductors:

"I remember one operator wrapping up his films in brown paper and string, taking it up the stair and sticking it under the seat when the conductor came up. 'Fares please' he says. 'Oi, what's this?' 'That's ma faither's tobacco!' "

In some instances, the assistants in the projection box would get roped into creating sound effects for the silent films. Although the orchestras could be quite inventive, at times a little extra something was needed over and above the knocking together of coconut shells for horses' hooves. Bob Douglas, spool boy in the Waverley, Shawlands, remembers some of the ingenious effects they created for a dramatic film of pioneer wartime aviators.

"There was this picture called *Hell's Angels* when we took the blades off the electric fan and put leather straps on, about six inches long and an inch wide. And we'd start up the fan and it starts revolving, hitting a tom-tom, giving an aeroplane effect. So if an aeroplane goes zooming — it was our planes in World War I — we played this and everybody thought the aeroplanes were going brrr, brrr, brrr, and we crashed the cymbals for the planes falling to the ground. And we got ninepence (4½p) for that because it was extra work."

With the number of cinemas in close proximity to each other in the towns, it was possible, indeed sometimes necessary, to share one copy of a film between them. This happened relatively infrequently with the nine or ten reel features, but was quite common with the newsreels. Johnny Mulhearn as chief projectionist was responsible for contacting his counterpart a few streets away every Monday and Thursday to arrange the timings of their programmes. This would allow the spool boy to take the newsreel off the projector when it had been shown in the first cinema, rewind it, put it into a box and set off at top speed round the corner to the other cinema. Johnny's spool boy was lucky: sometimes lads facing longer journeys and unable to get on to the trams performed an Olympian sprint along the road or pedalled furiously on their bikes to get there on time. They would be racing up the steps to the projection box with seconds to spare before the newsreel was supposed to begin. Quite a few operators recall slowing down the last reel of the feature film whilst keeping an anxious ear cocked for the footsteps on the stairs.

In the 1920s when synchronised sound had yet to appear, it was possible to control the speed of the projectors. This was a useful facility if it was a popular film and the house was likely to be full.

"When we had a queue outside, the manager would phone up to say 'go fast, there's a queue'. We went that fast the people couldn't read the sub-titles. They were asking 'What did that say? What did that say?' And then when we got the

queue in, I'd go slow to spin out the programme
to half-past ten and they could read the sub-titles
three or four times it was going that slow!''
Bob Douglas once put this experience to good use, playing
a prank on the orchestra which earned him the undying enmity
of the Waverley's band-leader.

"I was only sixteen at the time. We were
showing one of these bouncing ball songs, and
the orchestra's keeping time with it. Devilment
in me again, I speeded it up, the orchestra's going like mad trying to keep up with it!''

There was more to being a projectionist than just arriving
at the cinema and switching on the projector. Although experts
in their field, most projectionists were called upon to perform
a variety of other duties in the building, which would vary across
the companies depending on the size of the technical staff. In
the small halls, the projectionist could be required to do some
painting, repair damaged seats, check lighting and fans and maintain the generators and even the boilers. The big city centre
theatres would probably rise to a handy-man or boilerman, but
there was still plenty for the projectionists to do.

In the early 1920s, the arc lamps projecting light onto the
screen were fired by carbon rods that had to be hand fed — woe
betide the operator who let his attention wander and hear a roar
from the auditorium as the picture began to darken! With later
automation, it wasn't necessary to be quite so vigilant, but few
operators could yet afford to stand by idly and watch the picture from their "ports" in the front wall. Each reel lasted only
ten minutes and there was a constant flow of reels back and forth
from the rewind room, lacing up machines, watching for the cue
dot that would signal a change-over to the next reel and check-
ing the life of the carbons. There were always at least two men
on duty at a time, many putting in a basic 60 hour week in the
decade before the Second World War, cooped up in a tiny box
that in many picture houses was not designed for the task it was
to perform. With so many cinemas converted from older

premises, the projectors were often squeezed into tiny cramped
rooms. The heat and fumes from the machines could make the
atmosphere in the box quite unpleasant and at times very
dangerous when considering the perils presented by the inflammable nitrate film stock used until the 1950s.

Some of these iniquities were dealt with after legislation in
1930 on safety in cinemas. Some smaller halls simply could not
afford to make the necessary alterations and had to close. The
legislation had been prompted by the Glen Cinema disaster in
Paisley on Hogmanay 1929, when some of the inflammable
nitrate film had apparently caught fire. There was, in fact, no
danger to the cinema, but somebody in the hall saw smoke,
shouted "Fire" and in the ensuing panic, some seventy-two
children were suffocated in the rush to escape from the cinema.
With cruel irony, most of the casualties were found piled up
against a locked fire exit — the locks being put on to stop
youngsters trying to sneak into the cinema without paying.

The projectionists' trade union NATKE (the National
Association of Theatrical and Kine Employees) had from its inception at the height of the music hall's popularity been concerned
with safety in theatres, and latterly cinemas. Lobbying by the
Union had done much to convince the authorities of the necessi-
ty for the Cinematograph Act of 1909 which came into force the
following year, drastically reducing the risk of fire in venues then
showing pictures. The Union, however, lost its impetus in the
boom years of the 1920s and by the time it had recovered its
vigour, had missed many of the opportunities to negotiate from
a position of strength that the massive popularity of the inter-
war years would have afforded. During the Second World War,
however, NATKE campaigned successfully for War Increase
bonuses and for the inclusion of projectionists on the Schedule
of Reserved Occupations.

But they could do little for the individual desperate for promotion. There wasn't such a high turnover of staff in the box
as there was downstairs in the auditorium and there was often
a bottle-neck at the higher grades. Once promoted to chief pro-

jectionist, life was a little easier, the hours a little less tiring and there were more opportunities to work outside the box. There was quite a difference in wages between chief and second projectionist and many a second, finding himself working under a youngish man, would start looking for promotion elsewhere. If he was lucky and employed by one of the circuits, he might get a chief's post in one of the companies' other cinemas, the extra wages often compensating for increased travelling time or wholesale uprooting of the family.

Alternatively, there was a chance to move out and into the manager's role. Many projectionists were given the opportunity to transfer to front-of-house positions, some more easily than others, depending on individual company policy. This "promotion" was often taken out of a sense of frustration rather than desire. Certainly for the chief, it held little attraction. He might have two afternoons and two evenings off a week, whereas the managerial staff usually just had one day a week, and the public relations side of the job often had little appeal to the technician who had trained in electrical skills and was proud of his standard of presentation. With the consolidation of the circuits, and as the trade began to shrink after the war, many of the chiefs became technical supervisors for a number of cinemas and found that they could keep in touch with their skills, but were no longer confined to the operating box for most of the hours of the working day.

Although it was undoubtedly much harder work then than today with computers and monitors to aid the lone projectionist in the cinema, there was a fierce pride amongst operators in presenting a first class show. Because so much relied on the vigilance and competence of the man behind the machine, there was much more margin for error and, generally speaking, the projectionist was conscious of the importance of doing a good job and the impression that it made on the audience. A picture hall's reputation was in some ways in the hands of the technical staff and they responded by endeavouring to put the brightest and sharpest image possible onto the screen. The profession had come a long way from the early days of the penny gaffs when dim flickering pictures appeared on painted walls and the matinee regulars began their monotonous chant, "Down a bit, down a bit, up a bit, up a bit..!"

# 4) "TALKIES"— TRIALS AND TRIBULATIONS

Ask any older picture-goer for their most vivid memory of cinema and it's probably watching their first "Talkie" film. For the projectionists who had to show these films, however, there were mixed feelings about the coming of sound.

Not that it was brand new by any means. For as long as there had been moving pictures, there had been attempts to produce sound and music to match. The early mechanical recordings, generally described as "singing pictures", were largely ineffective however, as they pre-dated developments in techniques of amplification that were necessary if anyone more than three rows back was to be able to hear! As the late George Kemp recalls of the family's early touring days:

> "We had talking pictures in 1907. The film was run through the machine and it had a gramophone with it. The sound was amplified by compressed air. You had a blower which went into one of these trumpet things and the idea was to get the film and the gramophone to synchronise with each other, which wasn't always easy. One of the records we had was Harry Lauder singing 'I Love A Lassie' ".

Although the compressed air system was at least audible throughout most of the old booths, these early singing pictures didn't last. The phonograph recording disappeared from the scene prior to the First World War and apart from one or two isolated attempts at improvements, they didn't really stage a comeback until the late 1920s.

Scotland, and Aberdeen in particular, can lay claim to a unique system of "real" talking pictures which was being advertised as early as 1908, and for a number of years was the only place in the country where they could be heard. The inspiration behind them was Dove Paterson, an elocutionist, who saw the possibility of combining his fine speaking voice with the story on the screen. He began in a small way, showing films such as *The*

New Talkie apparatus installed in the Playhouse, Peterhead. The gramophone discs were placed on the turntables at the rear of each machine.

*Rarebit Fiend* and *Oh, What A Night After A Fish Supper* and as "conductor" he guided his audience through the story. His technique developed quickly and by 1908 he had opened a permanent cinema, the Gaiety in Aberdeen's Shiprow. Here he advertised his "real" talking pictures. He would stand behind the screen and shout out an impromptu dialogue to fit the story. Later, by employing a lady to do the female and children's voices and by creating ingenious sound effects for the background, he provided for Aberdonians a rare preview of what was to be in store for cinema-goers of a later generation.

There were other sporadic attempts to bring live sound to the pictures in the years to follow. Bob Douglas recalls the night Father O'Flynn visited the Waverley:

> "He brought his film with him and he sang along with the orchestra, miming the fellow up on the screen and his wife was up in the projection room telling us when to go slow or speed up. It only lasted about three quarters of an hour, but the public took to it."

The public certainly took to the Talkies when they arrived for good in the late 1920s, but they probably had little notion of the effect they caused upstairs in the box. Projectionists felt that they already had enough on their hands without the added burden of this new technological advancement. One apprentice returning from his annual fortnight's holiday discovered that the cinema had been equipped for sound during his absence.

> "I came back on the Monday morning and I saw all this. It was the records at first. And I had one look at the place and I said 'I'll be out of here by the end of the week.'" (Although Alec Davidson did stay on and subsequently became a chief projectionist.)

For the first year or so, the new synchronised sound was produced from a large gramophone disc mounted on a turntable at the rear of the projector. The theory was that both film and disc would start at the same time when the machine was switched on.

One side of a disc corresponded to one reel of picture. The records played from the centre out with an arrow indicating where the needle should be placed at the start.

> "The beginning of your reel said Start Here and you put that in the centre of your gate and the needle on the record and that way you were synchronised. A couple of frames out and it was very funny. It was what we called out-of-synch."

As Bob Douglas remembers, the problems were many and varied.

> "We were showing Norma Shearer in *The Trial of Mary Dougan* and we changed over to the next reel and she said 'I will not, I will not.' And I thought she's saying that an awful lot. 'I will not, I will not.' The needle had stuck in the groove!"

Kept busy with reel changes, rewinding and maintaining the carbons, there was little time left to devote to the gramophone records. Bob recalls on one occasion picking up Reel 6 of the discs, lacing up the corresponding reel in the projector and performing a perfect change-over. Unfortunately, in his haste he'd picked Reel 9 of the discs and some confusion arose in the hall when the hero, singing to his leading lady, was heard loud and clear speaking with a woman's voice!

In the cramped conditions of the operating box, it was all too easy for accidents to happen. On several occasions, the operator's overall caught on the needle as he walked past the machine. Zzzzip! and it was back to the beginning of the reel again! It must have been a relief for projectionists when the new combined "sound on film" eventually arrived and took precedence. With the sound track running down the side of the film itself, there was no more need for the unwieldy and easily-broken stack of discs in the Rewind Room. There were fewer interruptions to the story as the operator, desperately trying to get the sound back into synch with the picture, gave up in frustration and switched over to the next reel, jumping several scenes on into the plot!

## 5) FILM TRANSPORT — THE BARROW BOY AND THE FILM TRANSPORT SERVICES

The introduction of sound discs must have seemed like the last straw for many a weary spool boy trailing down to the depot after the last house on a Saturday night. Transporting the heavy reels of film by hand was not easy, and the last thing he needed was another awkward parcel of gramophone records.

Glasgow was the main distribution centre for Scotland and most of the major film renters had offices in the city as near as they could get to the railway stations. John McCabe started as a barrow boy in 1926 with Ideal Films, whose trade slogan was "Sit back and enjoy an Ideal comedy". He went round the stations twice a day delivering and collecting films and then down to the Clyde steamer quays to off-load films for Campbeltown and Stornoway. He later moved to Warners and remembers their heyday with a big warehouse in the East End from which four hundred features a week would be put out to cinemas all over Scotland.

For the American companies who dominated film supply in the silent era, it was a boom time. Bill Grant, starting in the ad-sales department at Paramount's offices in 1926, received the princely wage (compared with his contemporaries in the cinemas) of £1.00 a week. He was responsible for keeping tabs on the flow of publicity materials that the renters provided for each film — the stills and posters that would decorate the cinema foyers and the synopses and press blocks that would be used by advertising agents to "sell" the film to the public. The exhibitors got to know what they could expect from the different film-producing companies and what went down well with their audiences. As Bill Grant recalls:

"Paramount was the top company at that time. You had the yearly agreement fellow who took your whole output. Now he booked those films a year in advance, sometimes they weren't even

"The Latest and Best in Talking Pictures" at the Empire Cinema, Clydebank 1930.

made, but he knew it was sixty-four pictures from Paramount and maybe only one or two duds. The rest he could depend on.''

However, the renters were jolted out of their sense of complacency in the summer of that fateful year of 1926 when the General Strike ground the country to a halt and along with it the railway network that had up until then been the major carrier of the films. The renters combined forces and took steps to counter the emergency using the experience they had gained in 1919 when the railways had previously gone on strike. In Glasgow, Pathe and Gaumont's offices were used as a focal point for the collection and distribution of films. The renters' travelling salesmen used private transport or whatever lorries they could find to carry films as far afield as Aberdeen and back. David Gouk, an employee in the Pathe office at the time, recalls those hectic days.

''I went into the office on Monday morning and I got home on the following Saturday. I slept in the theatre and films were coming in at all hours of the night, all hours of the early morning, and we had to feed the drivers, pack up the film and get them away back again. That was the beginning of the Film Transport Service. Brigadier Ivor Grove was domiciled in Broxburn and had a little carrier's business. He brought in the films from that area, Broxburn, Armadale, Whitburn, Bathgate, Uphall, etc. He had come through the picket lines of the miners on strike. When he arrived in Union Street, there wasn't a window in his car. But he had all the films.''

The Brigadier's experiences were not lost to chance. He saw potential for a challenge to the railway's former monopoly of film carriage and set up the company known as Film Transport Services that was to become the backbone of the industry for the

Wee Johnny the barrow boy, from "The Scottish Cinema" 1919.

next fifty years. As David Gouk explains, he provided a service that the railways couldn't compete with.

> "An exhibitor could now depend on receiving his films the same night as they were to be shown. The little places in Fife could have a matinee whereas in the days of the railway company, they couldn't, as they didn't get their films until 6 or 7 pm! It was a difficult job because they had to collect their film and deliver it back. Now all they had to do was to give their keys to Film Transport Services, who would walk in at any time, leave the films at the cash box and disappear. That was the origin of Film Transport Services."

And, no doubt, the fairy godmother of the thankful spool boy!

Charlton Heston visiting Glasgow to promote "THE GREATEST SHOW ON EARTH" 1952. Bill Grant, bottom right, and colleagues from Paramount's Glasgow office pose with him.

Queue for the Mickey Mouse Club, Scotland's first, at the New Tivoli, Edinburgh 1936.

# PART 4. THE PATRON'S VIEW

## 1) MATINEES — "HEY MISTER, SKOOSH ME!"

"Saturday nights — you always had to stand in a queue."
Such was the popularity of picture-going in its golden era. Every
cinema from sumptuous picture palace to local "bug hut" would
be assured of a full house on Saturday. Such was the confidence
of some cinema-goers in the standard of film entertainment in
those days that sometimes, on a busy night and particularly if
it was raining, a couple would choose the picture house with the
shortest queue and take their chance on the film they were waiting
to see! Nine times out of ten they would not be disappointed.

For nigh on three decades, the pictures played a central part
in many people's leisure time, not a few growing up with the
cinema from their infant years and continuing to derive as much
pleasure from the experience well into middle age. The success
of cinema in those days cannot be attributed to just one or two
factors. It was a blending together of many different aspects of
life that fused into a unique experience. For some it was purely
and simply escapism. A place to go where for a few hours at least
you could lose yourself in the drama or romance of a different
set of lives and a world totally divorced from the reality outside.
In the particularly lean years of the Depression, the picture houses
provided a warm comfortable atmosphere where everybody tried
to put aside their personal difficulties for a while and indeed for
some it even made economic sense. With no wages coming into
the household, it was often cheaper to take the whole family to
the local cinema rather than spend the price of admission on a
bag of coals for the fire at home.

For those alone in the world, the cinema was contact with
the community outside the home. The manager was a friend who
would always stop to have a word with you on the way in and
would take the trouble to enquire after your health had you missed
a regular visit to the cinema. It was a meeting place for old friends
where you could all enjoy the community singing in the interval
and in some cases, a cup of tea and a biscuit during the show.
Some of the palaces of the 1920s had tearooms adjacent to the
auditorium where it was considered fashionable to take tea whilst
watching the film. With the introduction of Talkies, however,
these salons had to close during the performance as the clinking
of tea cups and the clattering of spoons was competing with the
dialogue on the screen!

For those with more catholic tastes, the city centre supers
with their full size orchestras provided high calibre musical
delights — often to the astonishment, if not ire, of fellow patrons
who had come to watch the film and could not understand why
some people applauded mid-way through the main feature.

Picture-going in its golden era was decidedly a family af-
fair, quite often on a regular basis and with the importance at-
tached to the outing, occasionally taxing the manager's skills at
diplomacy.

"On the Saturday night, one of the ushers came
to me and said, 'Oh Mr Gouk, there's a little bit
trouble. There's a couple sitting in this seat and
they won't move.' So I went in and I spoke to
this couple and asked 'What's the problem?' 'Oh,
we came in here first and this couple here want
us to move'. So, I turned to this gentleman and
his wife and I asked, 'What's the problem?' He
says, 'Well mister, we come here every Saturday
night and this is our seat and when Mr Harper
was here he made sure we always sat here.' So,
after speaking to the young couple, I got them
to move. But it was quite a regular habit in the
old days. People went to the pictures twice a
week, maybe on a Monday and a Thursday night,
and they liked to sit in the same seat."

It was perhaps children who got most enjoyment from the
pictures. On the whole more receptive to the fantastic stories,
to the daring escapades of the goodies and the unmitigated evil

of the baddies, they entered into the spirit of it wholeheartedly, identifying with their heroes on the screen. Children formed a large proportion of the average cinema's audience and exhibitors would often provide extra enticements to encourage the youngsters' regular visits to their picture halls. David Gouk has recollections of two cinemas in Govan.

"There was McLaren's Picture House and across the road there was Jimmy Hamilton's Helen Street Picture House. And the children would roll up, and in those days there was no radio, no nothing, and the matinee, the Saturday matinee, was the highlight of the week. So you have three or four hundred children on one side of the street, four or five hundred on the other side and Jimmy Hamilton would come out with sticks of rock and he would wave them — 'Sticks of rock. Into the pictures.' And the kids would rush across the street. And the next week it would be the other manager's turn and he would come out with strings of balloons. This battle would go on week after week, Saturday afternoons. Great fun for the kids."

It was fairly well on into the life of the industry before the specialised children's clubs were formed. For many years, the children attended regular programmes, usually claiming the 4 o'clock performance after school and Saturday afternoons as their own.

One of the pioneers of Saturday matinees in Scotland was J.J. Bennell, founder and sole proprietor of BB Pictures. He had been a salesman for Sidney Carter's pictures, travelling all over the country in the early 1900s prior to settling on Scotland as the home for his first picture show. He acquired from the Good Templars' Association a huge hall in Glasgow's Gorbals and from there in 1907 he launched his "Bright and Beautiful" Pictures. He recalled in later years that "All the prophets predicted failure. They were all wrong, as prophets often are". The BBs became staunch favourites with local children, some 3,000 of whom attended on a Saturday afternoon. Elizabeth Smillie is one of those who still remembers BB Pictures.

"It was just a big hall and all around it were windows. There used to be a man, a Mr Bennie (Bennell), who used to go round pulling down the blinds to shut out the light and, of course. we were all crowded in, hundreds of children. When he came to the last blind what a roar went up because we knew that the pictures would be going on. But no, he came on to the stage and it was then he led us in a song: 'BB Pictures, they're all right, Come and see them every night, we will sing with all our might, BB Pictures they're all right.' "

As an added incentive to picture-going, Bennell operated a sort of dividend system, whereby "if you attended regularly, you got a wee book and they used to stamp it. If you attended for a season, you got in free one day."

A stick of rock was included in the penny admission, so getting in for nothing once in a season was a real incentive to those working on a weekly budget of tuppence (1p) pocket money. All sorts of ingenious ploys were dreamed up to save money on the pictures. Katie Smith recalls the matinee at the somewhat notorious "Starry", a former church hall off Edinburgh's Canongate. It was her job to take the smaller children in the family to the pictures and to let her mother away to do the shopping.

"I always used go on a Saturday. The matinee was a penny and up on the wall as you walk up the stairs there was the box for paying and it said there that you didn't have to pay for a child in arms. So, I used to go with my wee nephew, Charlie. I was about seven, he'd be about three, he was a big fat boy too, and my sister and my wee niece and I would lift up Charlie, put him

'Merry children at Scott's happy matinee'' in a former wire works in the East End of Glasgow 1913.

in my arms you see, and I'd walk up, oh, I could hardly walk up those stairs because I was always a small thin person and I'd get up the stairs and I'd say, 'One.' And she'd say, 'What about him?', and I'd say 'Children in arms are not paid for!' 'Go on, away with you! In you go!' "

The Star was a basic square-shaped church hall with an entrance at the top of a flight of steps and one single fire-exit at the front of the hall beside the screen. Like many of their contemporaries, the youngsters would try all sorts of dodges to get in for nothing. Katie's brother was no less audacious than she was.

"My brothers used to like to go at night. They were older than us, you see, and they'd go with their pals, there would maybe be five of them, and they'd be about thirteen or fourteen. My brother Sam would go up to the house and take an old cap and shove it on his head, then he would go to the Starry and say to the man in the box, 'Ma Mum and Dad's in the pictures and they've got the key and I can't get in. Could I go in an' get them?' And the man would look at him and say, 'Alright, well, give me your cap.' It would be an old cap, Sam didnae care whether he got it back or no. 'Get in.' So he used to go into the picture house, intae it and right down the side and open the door, the fire door, and all the crowd were at the back waiting to get in and they were like ants, Brrr! — and the light would shine on the screen. 'Shut that door! Shut that door!' Of course, the man was down like a shot. He could never find them, there was such a crowd. And they'd be sitting amongst them, shouting 'Shut that door, shut that door!' — and they'd just come in it!"

The "Scratcher" as the Star was also known was never properly converted for pictures. A level hall, wooden, with tin covering the stained glass windows, its forms would fill to overflowing every Saturday and latecomers would sit on the floor at the front and squeeze themselves in down the sides till the place was jam-packed. It had virtually no toilet facilities and had earned a reputation for a liberal use of disinfectant on the poor unfortunates who couldn't hold out to the end of the film! Regulars at the Starry will no doubt remember the happy days at the matinee when every so often a small voice would cry out to the usher with his disinfectant syringe, "Hey Mister, Skoosh me!" The "Starry" was not necessarily typical of its kind. Indeed, with somewhat quaint irony, it was equipped with an organ long before its posher rivals up town, a legacy of the church's tenancy. The organist, to Katie Smith's never-ending fascination, had a wooden leg!

The matinee audiences had their heroes of the silver screen, whose daring exploits would be recreated by their small fans in streets and closes for days afterwards. Nearly every programme had a comedy and at least one Western. It was the days when the goodies wore white hats and baddies black. Minor scuffles would break out in the back stalls as the action on the screen spilled over into the ranks of supporters in the hall. Children would shout themselves hoarse warning their hero to "watch your back!" or cheering when the US cavalry beat off the Redskins.

When the serials began to appear about the time of the First World War, the highlight of the week was finding out how Lieutenant Daring was to outwit the insidious foreigner and if the heroine of the *Exploits of Elaine* would escape death from the oncoming train! These and many other serials kept the matinee audiences on the edge of their seats for week after week, never failing to convince them of impending danger "To be continued next week!" The programme was packed with action and could be guaranteed to leave the participants exhausted at the end of the show.

The tradition of variety overlapped cinema for quite a number of years into its life. Originally, vaudeville "turns" were employed to fill in the gaps between films where there was only one projector. The "turns" were quite commonplace within the cinema programme and although largely phased out by the era of big picures, they still had a place in the children's matinees. A cinema would run "Go As You Please" contests, a sort of "Opportunity Knocks" for local people. Katie Smith recalls the competitions at Pringle's Picture Palace in Elm Row, now the site of STV's Gateway studios.

"You'd put your name in and you went up. And, of course, if somebody from your street went up, you all went in to see him. You 'encored' him. They practised for a week before it. The first prize was five shillings and if you won, oh dear!, five shillings — you were millionaires. They used to practise on all the stair heads."

Scotland's first Mickey Mouse Club, a Saturday show especially for children, opened at the New Tivoli in Edinburgh in 1934. Before long, the children's club became a regular feature of cinema-going, the big circuits jumping onto the bandwagon. Each club had its own song, usually encapsulating very noble sentiments.

"We come along on a Saturday morning, greeting everybody with a smile.
We come along on a Saturday morning, knowing it's all worthwhile.
As members of the Odeon Club, we all intend to be,
Good citizens when we grow up and Champions of the Free."

Special programmes were devised for these "Champions of the Free", who would let the exhibitors know, in no uncertain terms, when their choice was unpopular. The girls at the Junior Club in Poole's Roxy in Edinburgh demonstrated through a chorus of boos and hisses that "under no circumstances would they like to see a Shirley Temple or Jane Withers film being shown in place of their usual six-shooting Western".

Saturday Afternoon at the BBs.

The Pavilion, Wick, hosting the world premiere of Neil Gunn's ''SILVER DARLINGS'' in 1947.

*John Adams*

## 2) THE CINEMA-GOING EXPERIENCE — FANS IN THE BACK STALLS

If conditions weren't always ideal in the local "scratcher", they could usually be bettered in the suburban cinemas that were purpose-built and designed for films. Several people recall the luxury of the padded tip-up seats when they appeared in place of hard wooden forms. Some, in the plusher palaces, had metal racks below the seat for placing a bowler hat. But not even the purpose-built halls could escape an environmental obstacle particularly prevalent in the industrial towns of the central belt. In the era before the smokeless zone, winter was the time for fogs, as Bob Douglas recalls, "thick yellow pea-soup fogs". They would slowly infiltrate the cinema filling the auditorium with a ghostly blanket.

"Well the couples in the back row didnae bother much, they were alright, they were enjoying themselves, but the ones in front were saying, 'I canny see the picture, what's the matter?' That yellow pea-soup fog used to come down every November until we had the clean air."

It must have been particularly frustrating in the silent era when the subtitles on the screen would become hazy and indistinct. There was always somebody in the audience who would persist in reading them out aloud, either for a friend or for their own benefit. With the coming of the Talkies, these unofficial commentators found themselves out of a job!

Considering all the previous attempts at talking pictures, particularly the appearance of De Forest's Phonofilms in 1926, it is surprising that *The Singing Fool* figures so largely in cinemagoers' recollections of their youth spent in front of the silver screen. Certainly it was one of the first full-length features to combine both dialogue and music throughout the entire film and heralded a new era in cinema. Most previous attempts at Talkies had either been dismissed by the trade itself or had failed to capture the imagination of picture-goers.

When *The Singing Fool* arrived in Scotland in January 1929 it was paired up with a silent second feature. By the second day of its run, the rest of the programme had been dropped and the "All Talking, All Singing, All Dancing" marvel of the age was run five times daily to try to accommodate the thousands queuing to get in. With several rival companies promoting their various sound systems, it took a few years for the technology to settle down and for the quality of sound to improve. Jim Poole recalls his first experience with the new-style Talkies:

"The film was *Speakeasy*. It lasted an hour and forty minutes and I have never actually understood, or never did understand, more than about ten minutes of it and neither did, I think, the rest of the audience. It included a mumbling negro porter called Step'n Fetchit. And even with the best of sound you possibly had, nobody could understand what he was talking about."

The cinema programme provided a full and varied night's entertainment to suit all tastes. American feature films were universally popular with their glamorous stars and handsome heroes. Those who had crossed the great divide from silent to sound soon found fame in the pages of the film magazine like *Picture Show* and *Film Weekly,* their private lives subject to the piercing scrutiny of gossip columnists. The fans would watch every single picture they made and would collect posters and pin-up photographs. On rare occasions, screen stars would make personal appearances to promote a particular film, sometimes touring in later years with live variety shows. Laurel and Hardy toured Britain in 1932 appearing before thousands at Edinburgh's Playhouse and the Glasgow Empire, being mobbed wherever they went in each city. Stan Laurel indeed, was returning to his former stamping ground, having spent some of his early years standing in the wings of the old Metropole Theatre in Glasgow watching the acts that his father, as manager, had engaged.

Winnie Lees, a journalist and film critic, remembers meeting her first film star.

> "It was Dorothy Lamour about the time of the *Roads* films. She came to the Empire (Glasgow). I made a phone appointment to interview her at the theatre before the show and I remember being quite surprised because I had imagined that I'd be meeting somebody very glamorous, you know, and she received me wearing her curlers and an ancient old dressing-gown thing! She was very nice."

If American films were certain box office successes, it was unfortunately a different tale where British films were concerned. Usually relegated to second feature status, they never regained the lead from transatlantic competition in the interwar period. Government measures to bolster up the flagging British industry forced exhibitors to take a certain percentage of British product every year. The Quota system kept "rotten British pictures" on the screens when exhibitors would have cheerfully dropped them. Bob Douglas remembers a comedy that wasn't doing too well.

> "We employed this man with a belly laugh to sit in the hall and all he had to do was laugh — a good hearty laugh — ha ha ha! and people round about were affected by this and they'd laugh and later come out and say, 'That was a jolly good film.' He got two and six (12½p) a night for that!"

Like most film programmes, the newsreel changed twice weekly, trying to keep as up to date as possible with events of national importance. In the era prior to the domestic wireless, the newsreel reached a massive public audience who took delight in seeing, as opposed to reading about in the daily press, personalities and famous places. There were four or five major companies producing several stories for each issue, and each with a distinctive trade-mark. Paramount was "the eyes and ears of the world", whilst Pathe's cockerel crowded triumphantly from the

Queues to see "The Lone Ranger" in person at Green's Playhouse, Dundee, in 1958.

screen. For extra special occasions a whole newsreel could be devoted to one subject. Gaumont-British produced special commemorative copies of their film of the Coronation in 1937 which were subsequently presented in beautiful shiny tins to most of the burgh corporations in Scotland, with the instruction "not to be opened for one hundred years". The commentators became instantly recognisable, for example Leslie Mitchell, whose voice is synonymous for many with the Movietone News of the 1930s.

For those cinemas near railway stations or on main trunk routes, it was possible to get a rush copy of a newsreel straight from London only hours after the event took place. For the outlying areas dependent upon the steamship services, it was a different story. The Picture House, Campbeltown, got its newsreel cheaper than more accessible theatres, but by then it was usually twelve days old!

Another staple in the diet of films was the interest film or "short". This would cover any subject at all, occasionally a local topical of the "Come and See Yourselves" variety adopted so effectively by Harry Kemp in Saltcoats. For a while in the mid-1930s, a Scottish film company began to produce a series of these shorts for local consumption. Entitled *Things That Happen,* they had an item for all tastes and interests. No. 1 in the series opened with a dramatic reconstruction of the capture of bank robbers by the CID, visited a shoe factory in Kilmarnock, described the intricacies of creating the latest "Glamorous Nights" coiffure, and finished with an exciting, exclusive feature on natural science: entitled "Proof at Last", Scottish Film Productions proudly revealed the first film evidence of the existence of a monster in Loch Ness. Unfortunately, owing to the overcast and foggy weather, the picture was not as clear as they had hoped, but through the murky atmosphere, the monster was revealed, captured by the telescopic lens of the intrepid cameraman!

The film programme was continuous with shorts or advertising slides filling the space where the interval comes today. Sometimes one night a week would be chorus night where the

bouncing ball, marking out a rhythm along the line of words, helped the patrons to keep up with the songs, or the words of each verse would be scratched on to a slide and shone on the screen.

The social life surrounding the cinema turned it into much more than just a place to watch pictures. The orchestra, musical interludes and, to some extent, the talent contest, broadened the range of cinema-going experience. For example, it was possible to get live coverage of election results long before the small screen invaded the living room. John Boll, projectionist at the Kings Cinema in Glasgow, remembers the election fever.

"We used to be up all night putting the results on, making up a slide, who got in and who did-nae. They were on the phone all the time and as each phone message came in, we'd put it onto a slide — just scratch it with a pin or a match and you showed it on the screen. People would sit up all night. The band would be there playing and as the results came through, they were flashed on the screen. At the Coliseum, when a Labour man got in the red balloon would come flying over the balcony, and when a Tory got in, the blue balloon!"

A slide asking patrons to make suggestions for future programmes.

*John Adams*

Regal Cinema, Anstruther                    *K.S. Wheelan*

## 3) WARTIME RECOLLECTIONS

With the declaration of war in 1939, the quality of life changed drastically overnight. The black-out was declared and in a panic measure, the Government ordered all places of entertainment to close. Life came to an absolute standstill at night. Chiefly concerned with the spectre of bombing, the Government's measures were designed to keep people at home, where they confidently expected BBC radio broadcasts would replace the entertainment previously enjoyed in theatres and picture houses. The decision was reversed after about ten days, the Government listening to the arguments put forward by trade and public bodies alike and from then on, the cinemas were to enjoy a boom period. The black-out still applied to the exterior of the buildings, however. The neon signs that had begun to make an appearance were switched off for the duration of the war. Illuminated facades remained dark.

For the cinema employees, it was a difficult time. They had to cope with depleted staff, shortage of materials and the need to maintain an overnight fire-watching rota. Some of the smaller cinemas just couldn't cope, closure forced upon them with the loss of two or three staff to the Armed Services. Others were replaced with squads of part-timers. In the spring of 1940, projectionists over the age of twenty-five were classified on the list of reserved occupations, but faced with the loss of their seconds and junior operators, they, like so many other workers at the time, found that the women were stepping into the breach.

Anne Harrow and her sister Jessie ran the films at the Regal, Anstruther, during the war years, performing their job conscientiously and with meticulous care for the equipment. The cinema had opened only a few years previously and the sisters remembered a beautifully furnished auditorium with rose pink carpets. Full attention had been paid to detail, the usherettes' uniforms being designed to match the carpet and "there was always a lovely smell of air freshener". Both sisters were trained to operate the projectors and had a boy to assist with the odd jobs. Anne Harrow recalls that the condition of the films during the war years was terrible and that they had to stand by the machine continuously holding the shutter in case of breakages.

Those long serving chiefs used to a well-trained staff may well have despaired at the situation, particularly when the women's approach to the job baffled them slightly. Anne and Jessie's "boy" certainly had no cause to complain. Trying to alleviate the rigours of food rationing, they brought in sweeties that they had made for him with National Dried Milk.

Few of the women remained in the box after the war. Most had to make way for returning servicemen and found themselves transferred to the cash desk or sweetie kiosk. During their spell behind the machines, they had had to cope with some of the busiest years the trade had yet experienced. Anne and Jessie's cinema was equipped with extra seats to cope with packed houses from the RAF camp and the radar unit nearby. Special shows for the troops were provided and in areas where there was twenty-four hour working in the mines, munitions factories and ship-yards, extra programmes were run in the mornings to let all the shift workers in.

The cinemas were packed throughout the war period. Rationing had restricted the way in which people could spend their money. They just couldn't buy as much food or clothing as they might have wished. Cinema-going, however, wasn't rationed and its resulting accessibility attracted the public in their thousands, desperate for something to take their minds off the gloomy quality of life in the black-out. As might have been expected, the newsreels of the period reflected the country's obsession with national security, omitting place-names or any information that might be picked up and passed on by the enemy's agents.

Richard Telfer, renowned for his musical interlude at the New Victoria in Edinburgh, and regular contributor to live organ recitals broadcast by the BBC, didn't anticipate that he too would be affected by the need for controlled information when he began his wartime broadcasts.

"For the first time, we'd to send in the music for what we were playing. This may sound ridiculous, but I remember querying with the engineer who always came up from the BBC, 'Why is this?'; 'Och, it's some business about codes they're scared that you're broadcasting!' "

As well as elaborate precautions to avoid confusion with hidden messages to French resistance groups, the organists were told that there were some musical effects they couldn't employ.

"We must not use any kind of bell. We'd cathedral chimes and all that. That was the signal, chimes, for approaching air raids in villages and so on. And so somebody in a little post office with a (radio) loudspeaker blaring away — they would suddenly hear these chimes — 'Oh my God! They've arrived!' "

At least some of the exhibitors recognised the contribution that their employees were making towards rapidly increasing box office returns. The Government was naturally taking its share through the imposition of the Entertainments Tax, but one company at least provided extra assistance for employees. Richard Telfer again:

"Rank was a splendid man. Every one of his employees who was called up received a sum of money each week. I got £2.00 a week which, considering in the army I was getting thirty bob (£1.50), was a lot of money. The four or five years I was in the army, that was sent to me in the form of a postal order every four weeks. It was a splendid piece of philanthropy on the part of J. Arthur Rank."

Indeed, the company began a superannuation scheme during the war and although employees hadn't contributed anything previously, the benefits were made available straight away. This philanthropic approach was not entirely new to the trade. Since

1924, provision had been made within the industry to provide for employees in financial or personal distress. The Cinematograph Trade Benevolent Fund had been founded to assist employees who for reasons of illness or personal misfortune were unable to work, or whose untimely demise might leave a widow or family in financial difficulties. Exhibitors, renters and theatre staff all contributed by providing their films, premises and services free of charge for special fund raising film shows. The CTBF opened a Rest and Convalescent Home in 1936 and over the years has received applications for aid from thousands of employees, whether in the technical, administrative or production aspects of the industry. It was a most successful example of self-help within an industry too young to have built up long standing, interest-gaining investments in its employees' futures.

## 4) THE JAM JAR CONTROVERSY — "IN FOR A PENNY, IN FOR A POUND JAR?"

It will not have escaped the vigilant reader's notice that so far no mention of jam jars has yet graced these pages. The subject raises such conflicting emotion that it has been avoided up until now. Was it really possible to get in to the pictures with a jam jar?

For every exhibitor who firmly denies this as a myth that has grown up with the industry itself, there is a corresponding patron who will categorically state that it was an integral part of their childhood at the matinee. Certainly no-one denies that old jam jars, taken back to the local grocer, would be worth 1d. or 2d. in cash depending on their size and that with the proceeds of this transaction it was possible to get into the pictures.

However, where fact and myth collide is the claim that it was possible to bypass the grocer and take the jar straight to the cinema, where it would be accepted in lieu of cash. Imagine the scene, however, the poor cashier tucked away in her tiny kiosk, facing a long queue of eager children all jostling for position and clutching a pound jar as if it were gold! Consider the problem it would create for the management. What would the cinemas do with all these jam jars? Where could they stack them until such time as they could be taken round to the local grocer? Perhaps, somewhere, there is a former cinema cashier who can actually recall an instance where they took a jam jar as entrance money instead of cash. If you exist, please lay this ghost to rest once and for all!

Paragon Cinema, Gorbals, Glasgow 1926. A converted United Free church.

*Strathclyde Regional Archives*

# EPILOGUE

Just as the meteoric success of moving pictures signed the death warrant of the Victorian variety houses at the beginning of the century, so in its turn was the mature cinema to face a similar threat with the advent of television into British society in the 1950s.

It was the Coronation of Queen Elizabeth in 1953 that really signalled the beginning of the end for the boom years of cinema. The industry, aware that audiences had been slipping away, had geared up for the event with special Coronation newsreels in Technicolor, hastily rushed to cinemas countrywide just days after the event. But the impetus was lost. Their thunder had been stolen by the small screen that was beginning to percolate through to British homes. Across the country on Coronation Day, set owners had their living-rooms crammed with neighbours and friends eager to see the event as it happened.

There was an ensuing rush to buy television sets and although the trade fought back briefly with the introduction of wide screen epics such as the CinemaScope film *The Robe* and novelties such as 3D, the decline had already set in. The challenge presented by television was compounded by the effect it had had on the Hollywood production industry, cutting back on the amount of films produced for cinema and starving the exhibitor of a choice of good product. The major circuits had first pick leaving little for the independents and smaller exhibitors, a proportion of whom, faced with stiff competition and lack of satisfactory product, were forced to put up the shutters. Epic films with wide-screen ratios and stereophonic sound were ironically to enjoy hitherto inconceivably long runs at the city cinemas still in business. Films like *South Pacific* and *The Sound of Music* reached large audiences, many of whom returned several times to see the same film.

The competition for audiences was stiffest in towns where several cinemas were trying to attract a dwindling number of patrons. X-rated films appeared on the scene as exhibitors began to pitch at a specialised market. With the emergence of "teenage" culture, the concept of family outings to the cinema began to disappear, although children's clubs were still popular with the pre-teenage group.

The plethora of large auditoria seating 2,000-3,000 patrons left the industry with too many seats to go round. Those exhibitors who couldn't get the product they wanted, in the wake of the Odeon and ABC's dominance of the scene, found themselves stuck with large cinemas becoming uneconomic to run, rarely attracting enough patrons to make financial sense. With the liberalising of the gambling laws, many of these second tier circuits turned their vast picture halls over to bingo, filling more seats each night than they had done for films. Many simply covered up the cinema projectors, shut the door of the projection box and secretly hoped one day that they might be able to return to showing pictures, instead of calling out numbers on brightly painted ping-pong balls.

It was within smaller communities that the independents had a higher survival rate. Caledonian Associated Cinemas, with its hegemony in the northern half of the country, had little competition from ABC or Odeon, most of their cinemas being in small towns never invaded by the big two. With some clout in terms of booking, they managed to keep open a higher than average number of cinemas. But like most of the smaller exhibitors they fell foul of the "barring system", whereby the major circuits playing a new film could bar any other cinema within a certain radius from showing it until their first run had finished. By the time the film became available for the others, it was usually "played out". One or two independents, by virtue of their geographical position, escaped this iniquitous feature of the industry. For example, the Picture House, Campbeltown, still going strong after sixty years, gets all the major films at the same time as city centre Edinburgh or Glasgow.

Now into the 1980s, cinema-going has radically changed from the heyday of the inter-war period. Smaller auditoria, highly sophisticated technical projection facilities and over-riding commercial motivation, make the cinema less of a special place in today's society, with little room for the individual. With its devotion to Dolby stereo, widescreen ratio, highly complex and imaginative special effects, it still offers escapism, but to a much narrower sector of society and without the cosy friendliness of years gone by.

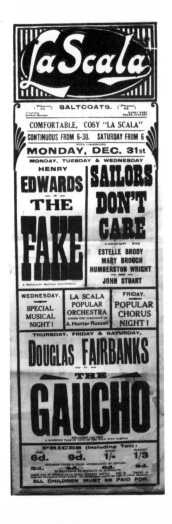

# ACKNOWLEDGMENTS AND SOURCES

The author would like to thank the following who have generously contributed to this volume by way of their personal recollections of the cinema in Scotland —

John Boll, Alec Davidson, Bob Douglas, Bessie Fury, David Gouk, Bill Grant, Charlie Hamill, Anne & Jessie Harrow, the late George Kemp, Winnie Lees, John McCabe, Johnny Mulhearn, the late James S. Nairn, J.K.S. Poole, George Singleton, Elizabeth Smillie, Katie Smith, Ken Smith, Agnes Taylor, and Richard Telfer.

— and to the many more whose stories, for reasons of space, could not be included.

In researching this book, particular thanks are due to Michael Thomson for information on cinemas in Aberdeen, Allan Eyles for his work on Oscar Deutsch and the Odeons, and to the family of James S. Nairn for access to his personal archives.

Most of the illustrations in this book are drawn from the collection in the Scottish Film Archive. Additional material has been reproduced with the kind permission of Kevin S. Wheelan, J.K.S. Poole, Brian Kemp, Bill Grant, the Scottish Record Office, Strathclyde Regional Archives and the Science Museum.

Thanks are also due to colleagues in the Scottish Film Council for support and encouragement in the writing of this book, in particular to Anne Docherty for typing the manuscript and Alan Crossan for reproducing original photographs.

Other written sources consulted include the following works:

*British International Pictures.* Brochure, Cornwall Press, 1930.

Eyles, Allen. *Oscar and the Odeons. Focus on Film,* Autumn 1975.

Heath, Syd. *NATKE: The First Thirty Years, 1890-1920.* NATKE, 1973.

NATKE. 75th Anniversary Souvenir Programme, 1966.

Oakley, C.A. *Fifty Years at the Pictures.* Scottish Film Council, 1946.
*Where we came in - The Story of the British Cinematograph Industry.* Allen and Unwin, 1964.

Perry, George. *The Great British Picture Show.* Hart-Davis, MacGibbon 1974.

Scottish Educational Film Association: Educational Film Bulletin 33, September 1946.

Periodicals consulted include *The Bioscope,* January-March 1915, *The Entertainer and Scottish Kinema Record,* 1913-20, (becoming *Scottish Kinema Record, 1920-22),* and *The Scottish Cinema* for November 1919.

Green's Playhouse, Dundee, decorated for the Coronation of George VI.

# Index